With an Everlasting Love

With an Everlasting Love

Selected sermons of

Rev Hugh M Cartwright

REFORMATION PRESS

Published by
Reformation Press, 11 Churchill Drive, Stornoway
Isle of Lewis, Scotland HS1 2NP

www.reformationpress.co.uk

British Library Cataloguing in Publication Data

PAPERBACK EDITION
ISBN 978-1-872556-14-7

© Reformation Press 2015

HARDBACK EDITION
ISBN 978-1-872556-15-4
© Reformation Press 2015

KINDLE EDITION
ISBN 978-1-872556-16-1
© Reformation Press 2015

PRINTED BY
www.lulu.com

Contents

Foreword

With an Everlasting Love is a collection of sermons preached by Rev Hugh M Cartwright during the thirteen years he spent as pastor of the Edinburgh congregation of the Free Presbyterian Church of Scotland, the closing years of his 42-year ministry.

Mr Cartwright's preaching was characterised by his gift for opening up a passage of Scripture in a way that did justice to the text in its context, while making its relevance to his hearers unmistakeable. Each sermon bore the hallmarks of the immense care he took in preparation – his sermons were invariably well structured, concise, informative, and pointed. He preached with unusual clarity, reaching through to the heart and conscience by the force of the truth itself as he opened it up, rather than resorting to dramatic tones or gestures. He was unflinching and accurate in his exposure of sin, whether in unbelievers or believers, yet his hearers were never left to go away discouraged or hopeless. Mr Cartwright very prominently and consistently preached Christ, as the Saviour from sin – not faith, and not experience, but the person and work of Christ himself. When he mentioned faith, it was faith *in Christ* and when he mentioned experience, it was experience *of Christ*. His goal in all his preaching was to make it obvious from his text what a suitable saviour Christ is, and how worthy of our trust, love, and obedience.

The present volume brings together a small sample of Mr Cartwright's sermons. It includes sermons on various passages of Scripture – some on individual verses, a series which works consecutively through the initial sections of 1 John, and a series on the theme of warrants for a sinner to believe on Christ for salvation. The volume ends with what turned out to be the final two sermons of Mr Cartwright's ministry. Although no claim is made that these are the best sermons he preached, they are nevertheless all selected on the recommendation of some of his hearers in Edinburgh.

The sermons have been transcribed verbatim from recordings, and then edited as minimally as possible to prepare them for publication (i.e., eliminating occasional redundant words, ambiguities and slips of the tongue). Some, but not all, of the many scriptural quotations and allusions are referenced in parentheses. Where verses were quoted with minor alterations to fit the context, these have been retained where appropriate rather than giving the exact quotation from the Authorised Version. In quotations from the Scottish Metrical Psalms, line breaks are denoted by a slash mark (/).

The publisher would like to acknowledge with gratitude the help of many individuals during the production of this volume. Meticulous transcription was undertaken by Catherine Hyde, Louie van de Lagemaat, and others who wished not to be mentioned by name. Catherine Hyde also ably assisted with editing. Thanks are also due to others who provided comments on a draft and who asked to remain anonymous. Matthew Hyde kindly provided the cover design. The publisher also wishes to thank Rev Kenneth Macleod, editor of the *Free Presbyterian Magazine*, and Rev Wilfred Weale for permission to use the obituary of Mr Cartwright first printed in the magazine as the basis for the biographical sketch.

It is planned that further volumes of Mr Cartwright's sermons will be issued, God willing, and the publisher will be pleased to receive suggestions of sermons for inclusion from Mr Cartwright's hearers. In issuing this volume, the publisher trusts that readers will be drawn more and more, as Mr Cartwright would have wished, to admire the Lord and Saviour Jesus Christ.

THE PUBLISHER
Stornoway
December 2015

Biographical sketch of Rev Hugh M Cartwright

Hugh MacLean Cartwright, the eldest son of godly parents Thomas and Margaret Cartwright (nee MacLean), was born on 22nd October 1943 in Motherwell, Lanarkshire, where his father was serving as a sergeant in the Royal Artillery. After the war the family lived for a short time near his mother's home in Dores, Inverness-shire, where his father worked in forestry. Shortly afterwards the family moved to Kennoway, Fife, where young Hugh's education began. In 1956, when he was about 13, the Cartwrights returned to Inverness-shire, where the rest of his early education took place, first at Glen Urquhart Secondary School and then, from the age of 15, at Inverness Royal Academy.

Although Mr Cartwright did not speak much about those early years of his life, it would appear from a comment he made at the General Assembly of the Free Church of Scotland in 1997 that it was in 1955, as he put it, that 'grace enabled me to entrust myself to Christ.' It was probably not too long after this that Mr Cartwright began to have thoughts about the gospel ministry for, when we follow his career after his secondary education, we find him embarking on six further years of study, three at the University of Aberdeen, where he took his MA degree in 1966, and then three more at the Free Church College, Edinburgh.

On completion of his studies, Mr Cartwright was ordained and inducted to the pastoral charge of Ferintosh Free Church in the Black Isle, in August 1969. There he faithfully laboured for twenty-one years, assisted by his like-minded, devoted wife Mina (nee Mackintosh), whom he married on 4th July 1969. These were happy years. Mr Cartwright's parishioners, including the writer, enjoyed a rich ministry, and the Ferintosh manse was a place of much kindness, encouragement and hospitality.

In 1990, a vacancy arose for the Chair of Church History and Church Principles at the Free Church College. Mr Cartwright's abilities and gifts were recognised and he was appointed to the professorship. Three years later he was also appointed to the position of Assistant Clerk to the General Assembly of the Free Church.

Everything would suggest that Mr Cartwright enjoyed those early years in the College, and his high quality teaching and warm pastoral care were much appreciated by the students. As time went by, however, the Free Church entered into a prolonged period of turmoil. In 1998, as the difficulties in the Free Church worsened, Mr Cartwright resigned his Chair and applied to the Free Presbyterian Church of Scotland to be received as a minister. While some may have thought that Mr Cartwright's leaving the Free Church and entering the Free Presbyterian Church was simply his getting away from a difficult situation, it is clear that this was not the case, and he never regretted the decision. As he wrote in a letter of February 1998, 'In God's providence the Free Presbyterian Church has been freed from the elements which were unhappy with her position and I hope that her unqualified subscription [to the Westminster Confession of Faith] will provide a rallying ground for others. The Formula [signed by ministers in both churches] is identical. The only additional question relates to approval of the 1893 Deed of Separation. A hundred and five years on, looking at it in the light of the situation in the Free Church today, I find it reflecting my own attitude to those in charge of the judicatories of the Free Church today, and have come to the solemn conclusion that, for me, the time to take this step has come.'

Mr Cartwright was warmly welcomed by the Free Presbyterian Church and was inducted to the vacant congregation in Gilmore Place, Edinburgh, in October 1998. The respect with which he was regarded within the Church was reflected by his appointment as Theological Tutor in Greek and New Testament in 2000. He also became a regular contributor of articles to *The Free Presbyterian Magazine*.

Although Mr Cartwright did not naturally possess a strong voice, his sermons were most carefully and thoughtfully constructed and relied for their force on the clear argument and warm experimental content of the message. Such a ministry was greatly appreciated in Edinburgh and in the wider Church. Under this ministry and his warm pastoral care, the congregation in Gilmore Place, which was largely made up of young people, almost trebled in size.

On 22nd September 2007 a shadow was cast over Mr Cartwright's life in the sudden and unexpected death of his beloved wife Mina. In a letter shortly afterwards he wrote of the great support Mina had been to him throughout his ministry. He also spoke of his congregation as having 'enveloped me in love and prayer'. This love continued to be shown in the years that followed, when the young people and visitors to the congregation would gather at his manse for fellowship after every Sabbath evening service.

Mr Cartwright contracted polio in childhood, which left him semi-crippled all his life. Despite this handicap, which became increasingly difficult latterly, Mr Cartwright continued in his diligent pastoral work and assisted at communion seasons throughout the bounds of the Free Presbyterian Church. He assisted at the Dingwall communion in August 2011. Shortly after his return to Edinburgh it became apparent that he was seriously ill. Mr Cartwright managed to take the services in his own congregation on 14th August. In the evening he preached on the words of Elijah, 'How long halt ye between two opinions?' and concluded with the urgent command of God to repent. This was to be his last sermon.

Soon afterwards he was admitted to hospital, where his condition rapidly worsened until, on 20th September, at the age of sixty-seven, he departed to enjoy the rest that remains for the people of God. On 28th September a large number from all parts and denominations gathered in Edinburgh for the funeral, where the grief that was evident reflected the fact that many felt they had lost, not just a minister, but a true friend and brother in the Lord.

REV W A WEALE
Free Presbyterian Manse, Staffin, Isle of Skye

1

With an everlasting love

JEREMIAH 31:3

The Lord hath appeared of old unto me, saying, Yea, I have loved thee with an everlasting love: therefore with lovingkindness have I drawn thee.

LORD'S DAY MORNING, 6TH MARCH 2005

As you know, Jeremiah lived at a time when God's judgments were coming on his people in this world. The true people of God among them might have been tempted to think that the Lord had cast them off for ever. Jeremiah was commissioned to deliver a message of encouragement to them, to assure them that the Lord would restore them to the favour which they had forfeited by their sin. The reason for that assurance was that the Lord's love is an everlasting love—the Lord does not abandon those on whom he has set his love, the Lord does not change his mind with regard to his purposes of salvation. It is that unchanging love, that unchanging covenant love of God, that is being set before us in these verses. The prophet is saying that the Lord appeared to him with this message, 'Yea I have loved thee with an everlasting love, therefore with lovingkindness have I drawn thee.'

It raises for us the question, whether or not a person can know that the Lord has loved him or her, and if so, how? How can a person know that the Lord has loved him or her? Surely such questions are of the greatest importance. Is there anything more wonderful than for a sinner to be able to say that God has said to him, 'Yea, I have loved *thee* with an everlasting love.'

1. Well, in trying to look at that, the first thing that we might consider is the everlasting love of the Lord for each one of his people. Jeremiah is one of them, but he's representative of them all. The Lord said to him, 'Yea, I have loved *thee* with an everlasting love.'

2. And then secondly we have the appearance of the Lord to those whom he loves. 'The Lord hath appeared of old unto me, saying, Yea, I have loved thee with an everlasting love.'

3. And then thirdly we have the drawing by which the Lord expresses and confirms his love. 'Therefore with lovingkindness have I drawn thee.'

1. The Lord's everlasting love for each one of his people

Well, first of all there is the fact that the Lord has an everlasting love for each one of his people. 'Yea, I have loved *thee* with an everlasting love.'

God is love. I suppose that is one of the best known phrases in the Bible. And it's a wonderful revelation of the being of God, the character of God, the relationship which exists eternally between God the Father, God the Son, and God the Holy Spirit. Supposing there had been no other beings ever in existence but God himself, it would be true that God is love. This is his essential character. This is the atmosphere, if we can use such a term, that prevails in the relationship between the three persons of the Godhead.

But not only is he love, we're also told in that same chapter in John that he is light. God is light. Where people go wrong is that they think when they have said God is love they've said everything that is to be said about him. Whereas in almost the same breath the apostle says, 'God is light.' Whatever else is in that wonderful expression, it's bringing before us the transparent holiness of God. The God who is love is holy. He is light as much as he is love. This transparent holiness characterises his love, as it characterises every aspect of his being. Therefore the righteous Lord who loves righteousness hates iniquity.

That's what makes it wonderful when we turn to the Bible and we find not only that God is love but that God *has loved*. That he has loved other beings. That he has loved creatures who are sinners. That's the teaching of the Bible. God so loved *the world*—he loved those who were in a state of enmity against himself, those who were alienated and enemies in their minds by wicked works, those who were under his wrath and under his curse. He loved sinners while they were sinners—ungodly, helpless, under his curse.

That is what the Lord is revealing here to Jeremiah, and to his people generally—'I have loved thee.' God has loved sinners. He has set his love on people who belong to this lost and ruined race. And this love is not mere benevolence, mere well wishing. This love is a determination to possess these people for himself, and to bring them into the most intimate relationship with himself, to shower on them all the blessings that are involved in him being their God and them being his people. That's what he comes to later on in this chapter, as we read, 'I will be their God, and they shall be my people.' And what unsearchable blessedness is in that relationship!—God being a God to us, and we being what his people should be. That is what his love is aiming at. That is what his love will accomplish. That's what his love *is*—it's this determination to bring these sinners into this most close relationship of harmony and blessedness with himself.

Now, it's when you think of the one who loves, and when you think of those who are loved, that you realise a little of the wonder of it. '*I* have loved thee.' The one who is speaking is glorious in holiness, the high and lofty one who inhabits eternity—a God who has no need of anyone, no need of anything, who is blessed for ever. All the reasons for satisfaction are found in himself. It's not that he needs the companionship of other beings. There's no deficiency in God, to be made up by others being brought into fellowship with him. He's holy, he's righteous. The prophet described him at the end of the previous chapter. 'Behold,' he says, 'the whirlwind of the Lord goeth forth with fury, a continuing whirlwind: it shall fall with pain upon the head of the wicked. The fierce anger of the Lord shall not return until he have done it, and until he have performed the intents of his heart.' (Jeremiah 30:23-24). This is a God who is angry with the wicked every day, who will turn the wicked into hell. And yet he is saying, '*I have loved* thee.'

And who is the object of that love? What would Jeremiah say about himself? What would he say about others who were the objects of that love? He would say what he has already said, 'The heart is deceitful above all things, and desperately wicked: who can know it?' (Jeremiah 17:9). 'That's my heart,' Jeremiah would say. And that's the heart of every one of the Lord's people, the heart of every sinner who's saved, the heart of every one whom God loves with an everlasting love—a deceitful and desperately wicked heart. 'The carnal mind is enmity against God' (Romans 8:7). Those whom God has loved are creatures, but they are *sinful* creatures, they are rebellious creatures, and they are creatures who want nothing to do with God until God persuades them to have something to do with him. What wonderful love that is! '*I have loved* thee.' A breath could blow them away into a lost eternity, but he has loved them and he has chosen them and he has purposed to save them and to put them in possession of life that shall never end.

That love of God for his people is obviously something that comes from his own initiative—something that is characterised by sovereignty and by free grace and mercy. What is grace? Is there any word that we use more often in connection with God's relations to his people than 'grace'? And yet, who can describe it? Who can understand this condescending love of God toward his people, purposing to save them from their guiltiness and save them from their misery and save them from their doom? It is sovereign, free love and mercy. It has no reason in us. It has all its reasons in God. That's what gives hope to you and me, that we might be found amongst those whom he loves—that no one ever deserved that love, no one ever merited it. Everyone who has been able to say, 'he loved me and gave himself for me' had to say also, 'I am altogether unworthy of the least of his mercies.'

You see how personal that love is. 'I have loved *thee*.' It's not love for everyone; it's love for *thee*. Some people take shelter in a notion of universal love. They say, 'God loves everyone, and therefore everything will turn out all right in the end for me.' But there's a very solemn verse in the Bible, 'Jacob have I loved, but Esau have I hated' (Romans 9:13). I'm not saying that there's anyone in the room of mercy who should come to the conclusion that God has hated them. Satan may be saying to some anxious soul, 'There's no hope for you because God has hated you.' No one in the room of mercy, no one under the sound of the gospel, no one anxious about their soul, has any reason to come to that conclusion. And may God give grace to resist coming to that conclusion in a way that would prevent a person from seeking the Lord and seeking his mercy. But what we can say is that you have no reason to believe the Lord has loved you until you're found embraced in that love in the person of Christ. We cannot take it for granted. We cannot say God loves everyone. 'I have loved thee' is something very particular, something very personal, and we cannot rest until it becomes particular and personal to ourselves. The love of God is a very particular, distinguishing, personal thing toward a sinner, so that a person has to make sure they have a reason for believing it with regard to themselves.

And one other thing about this love of God toward the sinner— he says it's everlasting. It had no beginning. With God, everlasting things have no beginning. God is the everlasting God. 'From everlasting to everlasting, thou art God' (Psalm 90:2). There was no beginning to God. We can't really grasp that. That's something beyond our understanding—someone who has no beginning. We can understand in a measure something having no end—we know that that's true of us. People try to blot out the idea of eternity, the idea of living beyond this world. But anyone who's heard the gospel—and even anyone who hasn't—when they listen to the underground noises in their own consciences and souls, they have this feeling—this fear, perhaps, this anxiety—that there's no end. Yes, there was a beginning, but there's no end. We can grasp that. But we can't grasp the concept of 'no beginning'.

And yet, God had no beginning. And God's love 'for thee'—for the child of God, for the sinner saved by grace—had no beginning either. It wasn't that there came a time in the experience of God when he began to love—no, God has loved eternally. Everlasting love. And that love is never withdrawn. It has never been removed from its objects. Even when he chastens them, even when he hides himself from them, even when they fear that the Lord has forgotten to be gracious and that he has shut up his tender mercies in his wrath—even then, this love is everlasting, it doesn't change. It's never withdrawn from its objects. And it has no end. It'll never come to an end. Its consequences, its effects, will never come to an end. 'I have loved thee with an everlasting love.' You don't need to be afraid that you were saved yesterday and you're saved today but that you might be lost tomorrow, because the love of God is not like that. As the apostle said, he was persuaded that there was nothing that could separate him from the love of God which was in Christ Jesus his Lord. Life could not do it. Death could not do it. Devils could not do it. Angels could not do it. Nothing can separate from the love of God which is in Christ Jesus (Romans 8:38-39).

2. The Lord's appearance to those he loves

Now, the second thing we notice is that the Lord appears to those whom he has loved. 'The Lord hath appeared of old unto me, saying, Yea, I have loved thee with an everlasting love: therefore with lovingkindness have I drawn thee.'

Now, of course, the Lord appeared to prophets in unique ways— in visions and dreams and voices from heaven—which he does not do in ordinary times to ordinary people. But Jeremiah is not speaking here uniquely as a prophet, he's speaking for the church. He's being spoken to as one of the Lord's people, and he's speaking as one of the Lord's people. The Lord has appeared to every one of those who have reason to say that the Lord has loved him or the Lord has loved her.

He appeared *of old*. We'll just look at this phrase briefly first. Perhaps he was saying that in the past, long ago, the Lord appeared to him. But I believe that what he is saying is that the Lord appeared to him *from of old*. That's where he came from—he came from the distance, he came from before time was, he came from the infinity beyond the present scene. It's the God of eternity who appeared, the

God who is infinite as well as eternal, the God who's removed from us not just in time but in distance of morality and spirituality. He's beyond us altogether. It's this God of glory who appeared unto me. He is not of yesterday or today, but from eternity. The God of eternity, who has appeared to his people down through the ages, he has appeared to me.

Now, the appearance of God is obviously a revelation of God. We cannot know God unless he reveals himself. We cannot know God other than by him revealing himself. By searching we cannot find him (Job 11:7). All the intellects in the world could never have discovered what we have in the Bible. That's why so many people won't accept it—they won't accept anything that they cannot reason their way into with their own intellect. Whereas the very notion of God is of one toward whom we cannot reason—we cannot discover him by our own experiments, by our own researches. He is the invisible God (Colossians 1:15). That means not just that we cannot see him with our physical eyes, but that we cannot comprehend him with our minds until he reveals himself and gives us that comprehension. Jesus Christ is the image of the invisible God. No one has seen God at any time—the only begotten Son, who is in the bosom of the Father, he has revealed him (John 1:18). 'He who has seen me has seen the Father also,' Christ said (John 14:9). He has appeared in the person of Christ. And that appearance has been recorded in the pages of his Word. It's in the Bible that God appears to sinners. It's in the pages of the Bible that we see his eternal purpose of grace revealed. That's where we see Christ revealed in all his glory as a Saviour. Of course, many a person has read the Bible from Genesis to Revelation and the Lord never appeared to them in the sense in which Jeremiah is speaking here. But the revelation is there. Everything we need to know is there. God in all his glory revealed is there, in the pages of the Bible. We're not going to get a voice from heaven, or a vision, to convey to us something that is not in the Bible. It's in the Bible we come face to face with God.

But when Jeremiah says, 'the Lord hath appeared of old unto me,' what he is saying is that the God who has revealed himself in his Word and in his Son, has brought that revelation to bear upon me in a particular and in a personal manner. The God who is revealed in the Bible, the Christ who is revealed in the Bible, the way of salvation that is revealed in the Bible, has been made a reality to me, by being impressed on my soul by the power of the Holy Spirit so that God in Christ is as real to me as anything I can see with my eyes or hear with my ears.

That's the reality of true religion. It's a different means of communication—a different method of communication. God may speak to us through what we read with our eyes and through what we hear with our ears, but there is this added element—he conveys to the soul by the power of his Holy Spirit the reality of these things, so that God becomes as real to me as if I had seen him with my eyes and heard him with my ears. The Lord has appeared unto me—he has impressed the reality of his being and the reality of the purposes of his grace upon my soul. I'm sure there's a lot more than that in what the prophet is saying, but there is that in it anyway. And there has to be that in the experience of any sinner who can come to the Saviour. That person has to have an experience which makes God real, which makes God appear to him.

You can think back on the effects of other similar appearings. For example in the case of Moses. Moses asked to see the glory of God, and what did Moses get in response to that? He got this word. The Lord passed by before him, and proclaimed, 'The Lord, the Lord God, merciful and gracious, longsuffering and abundant in goodness and truth, keeping mercy for thousands, forgiving iniquity and transgression and sin, and that will by no means clear the guilty, visiting the iniquity of the fathers upon the children, and upon the children's children, unto the third and to the fourth generation.' (Exodus 34:6-7). Whatever else there was in that, God revealed himself in his word. And that word conveyed to Moses the truth concerning God. 'And Moses made haste, and bowed his head toward the earth, and worshipped. And he said, If now I have found grace in thy sight, O Lord, let my Lord, I pray thee, go among us; for it is a stiffnecked people; and pardon our iniquity and our sin, and take us for thine inheritance.' (Exodus 34:9). You see the effect of the

Lord appearing powerfully in his word—it humbled Moses, and made him cry for God's mercy and God's presence.

It was the same with Isaiah, when he saw something of the glory of the Lord in the temple. 'Woe is me! for I am undone; because I am a man of unclean lips, and I dwell in the midst of a people of unclean lips: for mine eyes have seen the King, the Lord of hosts.' (Isaiah 6:5). And when the Lord appears to any sinner, when he makes himself known, effects like that follow. The Lord appears to those whom he loves. He makes himself known to them, he makes himself real to them, through his Word and by his Spirit.

3. The drawing which expresses and confirms God's love to his people

And then the third thing that we might notice is the drawing which expresses and confirms the love of God to his people. 'The Lord hath appeared of old unto me, saying, Yea, I have loved thee with an everlasting love, therefore with lovingkindness have I drawn thee.'

You see, when the Lord's love is communicated to a soul, that soul is drawn by his lovingkindness to the Lord himself. The love of God is not inoperative, it's not ineffective. The love of God is effective in the experience of the sinner—it has consequences which follow in the sinner's experience.

'We love him, because he first loved us' (1 John 4:19). If his love is shed abroad in our hearts by the Holy Ghost which is given unto us, then we will be drawn to him. That is what the Lord is saying here to Jeremiah. The evidence you have that I have loved thee is that with lovingkindness have I drawn thee.

Now, this drawing is a way of expressing what we know as effectual calling—God calling sinners powerfully by his Word and by his Spirit. To use the words of the Shorter Catechism, this is a work of his grace, whereby, convincing us of our sin and misery and enlightening our minds in the knowledge of Christ, renewing our wills, he doth persuade and enable us to embrace Jesus Christ, freely offered to us in the gospel. This is the drawing that is spoken of here—the soul being drawn away from sin and unbelief and enmity to God.

The fact that we are drawn indicates that we would not come without that drawing. No one ever came to God—no one ever came to Christ—who was not drawn by him. That should be an encouragement to anyone who feels drawn to the Saviour—that feeling didn't come from yourself, it wasn't your own initiative, it's the doing of the Lord. It's the Lord who is drawing you to himself. People don't come themselves. People come because they are drawn. They don't help themselves to come, either—they are drawn. Their desires, their endeavours, their prayers, their longings, are all expressive of the fact that they are being drawn to the Lord, by the Lord.

There's a passage in Hosea where the Lord amplifies this idea. He says, 'When Israel was a child, then I loved him, and called my son out of Egypt. I taught Ephraim also to go, taking them by their arms; but they knew not that I healed them. I drew them with cords of a man, with bands of love' (Hosea 11:1-4). I drew them with cords of a man, with bands of love. The Lord does not treat sinners as if they were animals, or as if they were machines. He treats them as human beings. He deals with them as rational creatures. There is an immediate, sovereign, powerful work of the Holy Spirit, which puts life into the soul of the sinner, but the expression of that life and the drawing forth of that life is through means, through arguments, through persuasions. No argument, no persuasion would ever cause a sinner to come to Christ without the regenerating power of the Holy Spirit, but where the regenerating power of the Holy Spirit is, God persuades the sinner to come to him—God makes him willing, God shows him the reality of spiritual things, God persuades him that there's truth in this matter. 'I drew them with cords of a man, with bands of love—I dealt with them as rational creatures, enlightened their minds, renewed their wills, convinced them of sin and misery, persuaded them, enabled them, to embrace Jesus Christ.' Any sinner who has come to Christ, has come because the Lord has drawn him, powerfully, by the work of his Spirit, and through the use of various means. Sometimes people did not know what was happening to them when the Lord began to work with them, and they began to see things in different ways, and things that didn't use to mean anything to them began to mean something to them.

But the Lord is also saying that he drew them 'with lovingkindness.' Lovingkindness was behind it, lovingkindness was in it, and sometimes it's the revelation of lovingkindness that draws the sinner to the Saviour. The sinner may be pursued by God's wrath, he may be afraid of the consequences of his sin, stirred up by a sense of God's curse to flee from the wrath to come—but what opens the door of hope, and what encourages him to hope for mercy, is the revelation of the lovingkindness of the Lord. There's mercy with God. He's waiting to be gracious. He's rich in mercy to all those who call on him. They see the love of God in Christ, and that draws them, it attracts them, to the Saviour. You see, different elements predominate in different people's experiences, and when some people look back, they may find that what was predominant in their experience was a sense of fleeing for their lives, fleeing from the wrath to come. Others may look back and see that what was predominant was the attractiveness of Christ to their souls, and the attractiveness of the love of God. There will be something of both of these things in the experience of everyone who comes to the Saviour, but the one may so predominate that the other almost fades into comparative insignificance. But however the Lord deals with people—he draws some of them with them hardly knowing what is happening to them—it's the lovingkindness of the Lord that accounts for it, and that is being expressed in the drawing.

And what the Lord is encouraging people to notice here is, '*therefore* with lovingkindness have I drawn thee.' If we have been drawn to the Saviour, drawn to put our confidence in him, then behind the drawing, we have to recognise the everlasting love of God. 'I have loved thee with an everlasting love: therefore with lovingkindness have I drawn thee.' The apostle Paul was saying the same thing in a different way when he said, 'Moreover, whom he did predestinate, them he also called' (Romans 8:30). Do you want to know whether you are elect or not? Then the question is, have you been called into repentance and faith and love to the Saviour? Has the Lord loved me with an everlasting love? Well, I can say, yes, if he has drawn me with lovingkindness, if he has called me effectually by his grace, and made me embrace Jesus Christ. I cannot see into the counsels of eternity, I cannot read what is written in the Lamb's book of life. But if I have been drawn by grace to the Saviour, then there's only one thing that can account for it, and that is, he has loved me with an everlasting love.

That is one of the ways in which the assurance of God's love can become the possession of a sinner. If you trace the streams back to their fountain, the lovingkindness which draws the sinner to the Saviour is a stream from the fountain of everlasting love in the heart of God toward his people. So, from that desire you have for Christ, that resting you have on Christ, you can trace back to the eternal purpose of God to save you. You see, it's not a case of finding out that he loved you, and therefore concluding that you will come. But if you come, you can conclude that he has loved you, with an everlasting love.

You see, it's much more difficult for some than for others to entertain this assurance, and that is why, I believe, the Lord is saying, '*Yea*, I have loved thee.' It is very emphatic. You may be questioning it. The devil may be questioning it. You may have your fears and your anxieties. But if God says, 'I have drawn thee with lovingkindness,' you can be sure he has loved you with an everlasting love. '*Yea*, I have loved thee.' He would have us to have strong consolation, as Paul says in Hebrews 6. He's confirmed it with an oath. He's putting all the power of the truthfulness of God behind it. If your soul is drawn to Christ, to God, to the ways of the Lord, it's the lovingkindness of the Lord that has done it, and it's the everlasting love of God to *you* individually that's behind it and that accounts for it.

Is there not great encouragement in this truth for the soul who is drawn to the Saviour? Encouragement to believe that, behind that perhaps feeble faith you have in Jesus, there is the everlasting love of God to your soul. You wouldn't trust him at all, if God hadn't loved you, and drew you in his lovingkindness. You're encouraged to be assured of his love, and you're encouraged to praise him for his love, and you're encouraged to rest on his love, seeing it is unchangeable. And let me just say it again, however feeble these movements of your soul toward God are, however feeble the grasp you feel you have of Christ is—if your soul is drawn to him and you're putting your trust in him, then you have to take account of the reason, and the reason is, 'Yea, I have loved thee with an everlasting love.'

And also, there's much here to stir us up to self-examination—every one of us. 'Do I have, in my own soul's experience, evidence of God's love toward me? Have I been drawn? Am I being drawn to the Saviour and to God?' Or, do I have to admit, 'There are no such drawings. There's nothing attractive about God. There's nothing attractive about Christ. At least, the attractiveness has not been such as to draw *me* away from the world and from my own self-righteousness, to the Saviour.' Well, that's a very sad situation for anyone to be in, and especially anyone under the sound of the everlasting gospel, who's been hearing the gracious calls and invitations of God's Word, and still has to say, 'They've never touched my soul at all, they've never touched my mind, I'm still without any real concern to have God as my God and to have Christ as my Saviour.' Is there not something here to provoke us to seek the Lord, and to seek these gracious drawings—to seek to be embraced in his love, as the Psalmist was praying, 'Remember *me*, Lord, with that love / which thou to thine dost bear; / with thy salvation, O my God, to visit me draw near' (Psalm 106:4)? Isn't it a wonderful thing that a prayer like that can be in the heart of a sinner—'Remember me, Lord, with that love, which thou to thine dost bear'? I'm not worthy of such love, but oh thy love is for the unworthy, the unlovable! Oh to be embraced in that love!

And where can a person be embraced in the love of God, but in Christ Jesus? The love of God is *in Christ Jesus*. As the apostle says (Romans 10:6-8), you don't have to go to heaven to bring him down, or into the depths to bring him up. We don't have to go in search of God or of Christ or of the love of God. The Word is nigh thee, Christ is in the Word, the love of God is in Christ, and the gospel is inviting sinners to come to Christ and to have Christ as their own portion. The devil will make you reason in various ways that will discourage you from coming to the Saviour, and make you feel, 'Well, if he loves me, he loves me, and if he doesn't love me he doesn't love me, and that's the end of the matter.' But that's not the way that God deals with a sinner. The sovereignty of God is proclaimed in the gospel. The love of God *is* sovereign. It *is* eternal. It *is* particular. It *is* distinguishing. But that love is in Christ Jesus our Lord, and the gospel is full and free in its invitations to have Christ, to come to Christ, to rest on Christ alone for salvation. And as I've said before, quoting others who have said it before us, 'If you are willing to have him, you can be sure that he is willing to have you.' That's the freeness of the grace of God in the gospel—if you're willing to have him, you can be sure that he is willing to have you.

May the Lord bless his Word.

2

Repentance causing joy in heaven

LUKE 15:7

I say unto you, that likewise joy shall be in heaven over one sinner that repenteth, more than over ninety and nine just persons which need no repentance.

LORD'S DAY EVENING, 14TH MARCH 2004

The parables in this chapter were spoken by the Lord in his own defence against the charges and the condemnation that were implicit in the murmuring of the Pharisees and scribes when they said, 'This man receiveth sinners and eateth with them' (verse 2). They meant that to be a reproach. They meant to imply that it cast some reflection on his character that he would be found in such company. That's a tactic that the Pharisees often adopted. They suggested that if Christ were pure and holy, he would not have been found in the company of such despicable characters as publicans and sinners.

The Lord is telling these parables to show just how false their accusations were. He came from heaven for the very purpose of rescuing sinners from their ruined state. When he was in the company of sinners, he was not there to condone their sin. The presence of Christ never comforted a sinner in his sin. He was there to confront them with their sin and to deliver them from their sin. He was the shepherd out looking for the lost sheep. He was the physician dealing with those who were sick and in need of his attention. He came from heaven to seek and to save that which was lost. He shows that the work he came to do is entirely in keeping with the principles of heaven. The fact that the Pharisees couldn't appreciate it just showed how out of harmony with heaven they were. If they had the spirit of heaven, they would have rejoiced to see sinners being converted and their lives being transformed and hope being given to them for eternity. So what the Lord is doing in each of these parables in Luke chapter 15 is showing that heaven rejoices when sinners are saved.

This evening, as enabled, let us try to think about this joy which is in heaven.

1. First of all, to notice what it is that causes joy in heaven. It must be something very significant that causes joy in heaven.

2. Then secondly, why this causes joy in heaven. There must be real reasons for heaven rejoicing at the repentance of a sinner.

3. Then the third thing is, what we on earth should learn from this fact that there is joy in heaven over one sinner that repenteth, more than over ninety and nine just persons which need no repentance.

1. What causes joy in heaven?

Well, first of all, what is it that causes joy in heaven? The Lord Jesus is the one who tells us that there is joy in heaven. He says, 'I say unto you.' He can speak with authority because he came from heaven. And indeed he was still in heaven, in his divine being. He can speak with authority about the condition of things in heaven. No one else can. We're dependent on the Word of God for everything we know about heaven, and we have to try to keep our thoughts about heaven within the confines of the Word of God, and not let our imaginations run riot, as they tend to do when we think about heaven. Our thoughts of heaven have to be regulated by what is said to us by God himself who reveals how things are in heaven.

Now what he says is that there's joy in heaven. Many people would be very surprised to hear that there is joy in heaven. It's not the view of heaven that people normally have—not the view they have of the heaven of the Bible. They have their own concepts of heaven, they have their own idea of what happiness would be, and in the case of most people it is a delusion. But the heaven of the Bible, the heaven where God is supreme, the heaven where Christ is central, the heaven where every creature is holy—for a sinner to imagine that there is joy in that kind of heaven goes far beyond the realm of possibility, because that's their very idea of misery. To be confronted with God, and surrounded with holiness, and taken up with Christ— that doesn't sound very joyful to a Christless sinner.

But the Lord is saying, there *is* joy in heaven. This place—where God is supreme, where Christ is central, where holiness characterises every being that exists there—is a place that is full of joy, full of blessedness. And what else could it be, when you think of heaven, when you think of God, who is blessed for ever—God who is characterised by infinite and eternal satisfaction and delight—when you think of the joy, the delight, the pleasure, which Father, Son, and Holy Spirit find in each other and in the fellowship they have with each other? Isn't that joy of the highest kind? Isn't that blessedness indeed? And that's what is at the centre of heaven. A God who is blessed for ever, a God who is eternally happy.

And all the creatures that are in heaven are joyful and blessed also. We're told about the angels that, when creation took place, 'the sons of God shouted for joy' (Job 38:7). We're told, when Christ came into this world, when the Son of God became incarnate, the angels informed the shepherds amidst shouts of joy. 'The angel said unto them, Fear not: for, behold, I bring you good tidings of great joy, which shall be to all people. For unto you is born this day in the city of David a Saviour, which is Christ the Lord. And this shall be a sign unto you; Ye shall find the babe wrapped in swaddling clothes, lying in a manger. And suddenly there was with the angel a multitude of the heavenly host praising God, and saying, Glory to God in the highest, and on earth peace, good will toward men.' (Luke 2:10-14). These angels are full of awe in the presence of God. These angels are characterised by reverence and godly fear. But there is nothing miserable about them. Because of their godliness, because of their reverence, because of their dwelling in the presence of God, they are eternally blessed.

So it is with those who get to heaven from this world. They enter into the joy of their Lord, the full enjoyment of God to all eternity, the full enjoyment of what began in their souls when they received the atonement. 'We joy in God through our Lord Jesus Christ, by whom we have now received the atonement' (Romans 5:11). There's something of that satisfaction with God in the souls of his people in this world. But oh what a fulness when they get to glory! Yes, there's joy in heaven, emanating from God, who is himself blessed for ever, and centring on God. Real, substantial, eternal joy, shared by all the inhabitants of heaven to the fulness of their capacity.

But the Lord is telling us here about something that contributes to that joy. It's something that happens on earth. 'Joy shall be in heaven over one sinner that repenteth, more than over ninety and nine just persons which need no repentance.' Something on earth causes joy in heaven. That shows the interest that heaven has in the things that are happening on the earth. It shows that there is information in heaven regarding matters that occur on earth. People wonder at things like that. Man himself can communicate in an instant with someone at the other end of the earth, but he doesn't think that God can convey to the people in heaven what is happening on the earth—but he can, and he does. According to the Lord himself, heaven has an interest in what is taking place on earth.

But heaven's estimate of what is taking place on earth is very different from the estimate that people on the earth themselves may have of the comparative importance of events. There's not a glimmer of joy in heaven over the things that make the hearts of men rejoice in this world. The earthly, material things, the things that make them so happy, don't affect the inhabitants of heaven. The things that fill the media as great and significant events in this world make no impression on heaven. But things that the world would never consider *do* make that impression. The conversion of a sinner—a poor, obscure sinner in a poor, obscure place, perhaps—causes joy in heaven.

Now the comparison made here is between one sinner that repents and ninety nine just persons. Of course, the figures are just part of the parable, we believe—they're just showing that one out of a great number is highly significant to the Lord. It might be dismissed by others, but it's highly significant in the Lord's way of looking at things.

Who are these ninety-nine? Well, some people think it's referring to the angels that never sinned. Certainly, God is more glorified in the conversion of a sinner than in the preservation of the angels who never sinned. More of his glorious attributes are seen in the work of salvation. Other people think it's referring to the saints of God, those who are in heaven, or those who are on the way to heaven, who have already been brought to repentance. You see people explaining it in the case of a family, perhaps—there's a number of children, and one of them has been recovered from a very serious illness or has been rescued from imminent death, and the parents are so joyful over that—it's not that they've lost their satisfaction with the rest of the family, but they're taken up with the fact that one has been so wonderfully delivered or preserved.

But I feel that the 'ninety and nine just persons which need no repentance' are not real people at all, but they're people who *think* like that about themselves. This is their view of themselves. The Lord is making a concession. These Pharisees and scribes would think about themselves in that way—as just persons, who need no repentance. 'You are they who justify themselves before men,' he says to them in the next chapter (Luke 16:15). He speaks about those who are righteous in their own eyes, and those who are righteous in the eyes of their fellow men—'certain which trusted in themselves that they were righteous, and despised others' (Luke 18:9). There's no joy in heaven over any amount of people who are satisfied with themselves and who feel that they don't need repentance, who have a righteousness of their own. But there is satisfaction in heaven over the sinner who repents.

Now we have to ask ourselves, 'What is a sinner?' You see, that was a point that the Pharisees were very far from the truth on. They thought that the publicans and the outcasts of society were sinners. And so they were. The Lord did not deny that. But he makes it very clear, especially, I believe, in the parable of the prodigal son and his elder brother, that the Pharisees were sinners as much as the publicans were. That's because a sinner is a person who is alienated from God in his own mind. And the elder brother, with his self-righteousness, was just as alienated from God as the prodigal son with his lawlessness. They had both left the father's house in spirit. They were both out of harmony with the father in their souls, although there was a great difference in the way in which that manifested itself. Everyone could see the prodigal son was a rebel against his father's house. But here is this dutiful brother, and until he opened his mouth, no one would ever have thought that he was just as alienated from the father. Then it all came out—the dissatisfaction, the self-pity, the self-righteousness of the man—when he was confronted by the grace of his father toward the prodigal son.

The Lord is teaching that, yes, those who go off the rails are sinners—but so are those whose hearts are alienated from God and who are righteous in themselves and who are rejecting the grace of God in the gospel. Sin is a deeper thing than the outward life. The outward life is very important, but there is a depth to the sinner—there's a 'behind the scenes' in the sinner's life—saying to God, 'Depart from us, for we desire not the knowledge of thy ways' (Job 21:14). That is what it is to be a sinner, primarily—to be *against God*. The carnal mind is enmity against God (Romans 8:7).

These parables are showing in different ways the character of the sinner—the stupidity of the sinner in the sheep that has gone astray, the worthlessness of the sinner as far as fulfilling his purpose in life is concerned in the coin that was lost, the wickedness of the sinner in the deliberate departure from the father's house that characterised the prodigal son. They're all pointing to the sinfulness of sin and to the awful consequences which sin has for the sinner. A sinner is one who has departed in heart from God, and who has come under the displeasure of God on account of his sin.

Now the Lord is speaking about a sinner that repenteth. We're all sinners. There's none righteous, no, not one (Romans 3:10). But there are sinners who repent. There are sinners who are brought to realise the error of their ways and who return to God. Repentance is a radical change of mind. It comes to expression in a change of character and in a change of life. There are two very common words for repentance in the New Testament. One of them concentrates on repentance as sorrow and carefulness, concern about one's sin. The other of them, which we have here, is more comprehensive—it's referring to the entire change that takes place in the soul and in the life of the penitent sinner. Sinners repent. Repentance unto life is a saving grace. It something that is wrought in the soul by God. The significant thing about repentance is that it's a turning *to God*—a turning to God from idols, a turning to God from sin. *God* becomes the great reality to the repenting sinner. The God who was despised, the God who was forgotten, the God who was rebelled against—he becomes *God* to the person. He becomes a reality to the person.

And because of that, the sinner comes to see his sin in a true light—he has a true sense of sin, something he never had before. He can honestly say, 'Against thee, thee only, have I sinned, and done this evil in thy sight' (Psalm 51:4). He can confess it, so that God's justice will be manifested in his anger with him for that sin. He has a *true* sense of sin—seeing it against God, seeing as meriting God's wrath and God's curse. But as well as having a true sense of sin, as our catechism reminds us, he has an apprehension of the mercy of God in Christ. How could a person with a true sense of sin turn to God, if all he could see was the holiness and justice and wrath of Jehovah? Surely he'd be fleeing from his presence, calling upon the hills and rocks to fall on him and to hide him from the presence of God, from the wrath of the Lamb! But what draws him to God, what encourages him to turn to God, is that he has got a glimpse of his mercy.

You see, the prodigal son must have had that. He came to see his sin in its proper light: 'I've sinned against heaven, and in thy sight.' But he was saying, 'I will go and I will ask him to make me one of his hired servants.' He believed there was an opening in the father's house for him, whatever position it might be—there was *hope* that the father would receive him. And that's in repentance—an apprehension of the mercy of God in Christ Jesus encouraging the poor sinner to turn to God.

And then, we're told in the catechism, that it's with grief and hatred of his sin. 'I'm ashamed of myself,' is the language of the penitent sinner. 'I'm not worthy to be called thy son.' There's grief and there's hatred of sin. Sin has become a horrible and a hateful thing to the penitent soul. The soul wants to be rid of it—the soul is ashamed of it. The soul is looking on sin in a measure as God looks on it. He's not sorry for himself, he's sorry for his sin. Many people seem to think that they're the victims—the victims of sin. No—we are the perpetrators of it. We are guilty of it. And when a person is brought to repentance, however sorry he may be for himself, he's not sorry for himself ultimately as a victim of sin or a victim of God, but he is sorry for his sin. He's sorry that he is a sinner. And he hates his sin, and he wants to be rid of his sin—that's why he's turning to God—to be forgiven, and to be changed. Because what he has in view, again as the catechism says, is full purpose of, and endeavour after, new obedience. He doesn't just want his sin to be forgiven, but wants to be delivered from its power—to be made a new creature, to have this new obedience that springs from a new heart, from new motivation—obedience that is always fresh because it comes from love to God.

'A sinner that repents'—a sinner who has been brought to think of his condition, and to turn from all his sin, to God. The Lord Jesus is saying, there's joy in heaven over one sinner that repenteth. There's no joy over those who think they don't need any repentance, those who parade their own righteousness. But when a sinner repents, there is joy in heaven.

2. Why is there joy in heaven when a sinner repents?

We have to ask now why this causes joy in heaven. Well, we believe that there is joy in heaven over one sinner that repents just because heaven is a world of love and of benevolence. Heaven sees the repentant sinner as a *saved* sinner. Some people on earth think a person can repent and yet be lost—but they know better in heaven. They know there that when a sinner repents, when a sinner comes to Christ, that sinner is on the way to heaven, and that sinner will *come* to heaven. Repentance is God's gracious work in the soul, and that repentance will never be repented of. The repentant sinner will never go back—repentance will continue in his soul till he gets to glory—he'll never perish, no one will ever pluck him out of Christ's hand. And heaven, being a world of love, rejoices at the repentance of the sinner because it sees that here is another soul rescued from going down to the pit of destruction, another soul on the way to heaven, a place prepared in the Father's house for him.

You see, what a contrast to hell! There's no benevolence there. There's no love there. You see that in the next chapter—the rich man in hell in torments wanting a message to be sent to his brethren. Oh, you would think, then there must be a spark of benevolence? But there's not a spark of benevolence in his soul. He doesn't want his companions in crime to become his companions in a lost eternity to add to his misery. There's no interest in anyone else in a lost eternity. It's a dreadful place, where sinners are given over to the enmity that is in their hearts against God and the enmity that will be breaking out against every creature with whom they come in contact. It's full of hatred. But heaven is a world of love, and heaven rejoices at the prospect of a poor sinner being saved.

There are other reasons too. We believe there is joy in heaven over one sinner that repents because heaven sees Satan's purposes frustrated and defeated in that case. Heaven sees the encouragement that that gives to the church on earth. Is there anything more encouraging to the church than when sinners are converted to Christ, brought to repentance? It gives a new life, as it were, to the church, or to a congregation, when a sinner is brought to the Saviour. And there's joy because the perfection of the church is getting nearer. Here's another of them gathered in to the Saviour.

But we believe that the real reason—the main reason—for joy in heaven over a sinner repenting is that the repentance of a sinner gives heaven a view of the glory of God. God the Father, God the Son, and God the Holy Spirit. The angels desire to look into these things. They desire to look into the things concerning the salvation of the church, because they see there something of God's glory manifested.

For example, when a sinner repents, what is happening is the accomplishment of God the Father's eternal purpose of grace toward that sinner. 'I have loved thee with an everlasting love: therefore with lovingkindness have I drawn thee' (Jeremiah 31:3). The conversion of a sinner, the repentance of a sinner, is something that was provided for in the covenant of grace, in the purpose of God, in the love of God, from all eternity. When heaven sees a sinner repenting, heaven is seeing the purpose of the Father being accomplished in the salvation of that sinner, and heaven rejoices because God the Father is glorified in that work. It's because he loved us first that we come to love him, and heaven sees it like that.

And when you think of God the Son, the repentance of the sinner is the fruit of his sacrifice on the cross of Calvary. He purchased redemption and he purchased repentance for his people on the cross of Calvary. And he's exalted as a result of that death on Calvary to give repentance to Israel and the forgiveness of sins (Acts 5:31). You remember what it says in Galatians chapter 3: Christ has redeemed us from the curse of the law, so that the blessing of Abraham would come on the Gentiles, that they would receive the promise of the Spirit—the Spirit of God comes to work in the souls of sinners for whom Christ died. His death has opened up that channel of grace to the soul of the sinner. So when a sinner comes to repentance, Jesus Christ is seeing of the travail of his soul, and he is satisfied (Isaiah 53:11). And heaven rejoices because it's seeing in that sinner's repentance the fruit of the sacrifice of Christ on the cross of Calvary.

Then, when you think of God the Holy Spirit, and you see a sinner repenting, you realise that that repentance was brought about by the washing of regeneration and renewing of the Holy Ghost, which he shed on that soul through Jesus Christ (Titus 3:5-6). It wasn't the result of his own reasoning powers. It wasn't from some principle buried deep down in the human heart. It was by the supernatural power of God the Holy Spirit that the soul was brought to repentance. You see, you get this mistaken idea that in the human heart, underneath all the rubbish, there are buried feelings which are brought to life and the person comes to repentance. There's nothing in the human heart that will ever produce repentance. But repentance is brought about when God the Holy Spirit regenerates the sinner— puts life into the soul of the sinner—*gives* repentance to the sinner.

It's the work of God the Holy Spirit to put life into the soul. You remember how Paul was saying that to the Thessalonians, how he explained their coming to faith in Christ, their coming to receive the gospel. He says (1 Thessalonians 1:5), 'Our gospel came not unto you in word only, but also in power, and in the Holy Ghost, and in much assurance.' That's what made it effective, that's what brought them to repentance.

So when a sinner repents, what is happening is that the purpose and power of God—Father, Son and Holy Spirit—are coming to expression in the conversion of that sinner to Christ, in the repentance of that sinner and his turning to God. And so there's joy in heaven over that repenting sinner, because the repentance is the work of God and the repentance is glorifying to God. The sinner is commanded to repent—the sinner is called upon to repent—the sinner is encouraged to repent—it's the sinner himself that *must* repent, and the Word of God makes that abundantly clear. 'God now commandeth all men everywhere to repent' (Acts 17:30). And he promises them that if they repent they will not perish, if they repent they will have life everlasting. There's no doubt about that. The gospel says that to *any* sinner—if you repent, you will have life, you'll have the Lord's blessing. But when a sinner repents, it's not because of anything that was in himself that inclined him that way, but it's because God had mercy on him. And therefore heaven rejoices, because heaven is a place where the glory of God is the supreme consideration.

3. What we here on earth should learn from this

Well then, what should we who are here on earth learn from this fact that there is joy in the presence of the angels of God, that there is joy in heaven, over a sinner that repents?

Well, should we not learn from it *what a wonderful thing the repentance of a sinner is*? What a precious thing is an immortal soul! What a terrible thing is sin, when it ruins immortal souls! What a wonderful thing is the conversion of a sinner to Christ—the repentance of a sinner, the bringing of a sinner to God! There's nothing like it. It's the one thing we're told that happens on earth which causes joy in heaven. So how can we think lightly of our soul? How can we think lightly of sin? How can we think lightly of repentance, when the Lord's words here impress upon us just how significant is the repentance of a sinful soul? It's bringing home to us that there's nothing more important in all the world than to be converted to Christ, to be brought to God in repentance.

Is that our own view of the matter, as far as we're concerned ourselves, and as far as our fellow sinners are concerned? Sometimes people can be very pleased when people get on in the world, and no doubt there is reason to be pleased when people get on in the world. But it's very sad when people are pleased at getting on in the world, or at others getting on in the world, and they've no thought about how it is with their soul. What will it profit a man, if he'll gain the whole world, and lose his own soul? Or what shall a man give in exchange for his soul? (Mark 8:36-37).

And also, we should learn from this to *enquire as to whether or not we have the attitude of heaven ourselves*. That was one of the reasons the Lord told these parables and made these statements—to show just how out of harmony with heaven the Pharisees and scribes were. They couldn't appreciate the conversion of a sinner being a momentous event, because they didn't know what it was to be a sinner, and they didn't know what it was to be a 'sinner that repenteth'. And they didn't know what it was to be received by this man—to be welcomed by Christ. These things were all strange to them. They didn't have the love that's in heaven and they didn't have the joy that's in heaven.

We have to ask ourselves, do we have the spirit of heaven ourselves, so that we think very highly of repentance, this gift of God, the salvation of a sinner? And do we think very highly of it with regard to ourselves, and with regard to our fellow creatures? We should rejoice when sinners are converted to Christ, when sinners repent. Do we have that desire in our souls for the repentance of sinners? Do we have that joy in our souls? There was once a man, and when people would meet him and say to him, 'What's your news?' he would say, 'Good news.' Every day, wherever he met anyone, when they asked him, 'What's your news,' he would say, 'Good news,' and then he would say something like this: 'Christ Jesus came into the world to save sinners.' That was the priority with him. That should be our priority too, and our hearts should rejoice at the thought of a sinner being converted—for the sake of the sinner himself, and because the glory of God is manifested. It's the doing of the Lord, and it's wondrous in our eyes (Psalm 118:23).

But then, the last thing we would say we should learn from this is *what encouragement there is for a sinner to repent.* What encouragement there is for a penitent sinner, in this assurance that there is joy in heaven over one sinner that repenteth! You remember these remarkable words that we have in Zephaniah chapter 3, speaking about the Lord's attitude to those whom he saves by his grace: 'The Lord thy God in the midst of thee is mighty; he will save, he will rejoice over thee with joy; he will rest in his love, he will joy over thee with singing.' There is another, equally wonderful, verse there in Isaiah chapter 30. 'And therefore will the Lord wait, that he may be gracious unto you, and therefore will he be exalted, that he may have mercy upon you: for the Lord is a God of judgment: blessed are all they that wait for him. For the people shall dwell in Zion at Jerusalem: thou shalt weep no more: he will be very gracious unto thee at the voice of thy cry; when he shall hear it, he will answer thee.'

What an encouragement for a poor sinner, that the repentance of a sinner causes such joy in heaven! The shepherd rejoiced when he came back with his sheep that was lost and found. The woman rejoiced when she found the coin that had been lost. The father rejoiced when his son came home. And the families and friends and neighbours joined in the rejoicing. We might think it's a bit exaggerated, the shepherd gathering people home to celebrate the discovery of one sheep, and the woman, of one coin—but you see it's just the meeting of the reality and the illustration. No illustration without exaggeration can come to express the wonder of the grace of God—it's beyond any human cause of joy.

What an encouragement for a sinner, then—what an encouragement—to know that he'll not be rejected. 'All that the Father giveth me shall come to me; and him that cometh to me I will in no wise cast out' (John 6:37). The poor sinner is tempted to feel that he will be rejected. But there's joy in heaven over a sinner that repents. And that is meant to encourage us to believe that this man receiveth sinners and eateth with them—that he has never turned anyone away, and he never will turn anyone away, that comes through him to God. That's the freeness of the grace of God in the gospel. Whatever reason you have for not coming to Christ, do not reproach him by saying that it's because you're afraid he will not have you. The Word of God is very clear on the matter, that he will receive *any* sinner who comes to him—*any* sinner who repents, *any* sinner who casts himself on the mercy of God. He cannot do anything else—he has committed himself to it. The love of God the Father is behind that repentance—the death of God the Son is behind that repentance—the power of God the Holy Spirit is behind that repentance—and how then could he do anything else, other than receive the sinner who comes? This glimpse of heaven is not given to satisfy speculation, but it's given to encourage poor sinners on earth to believe that what the Pharisees said is true, although it's not a reproach but a glory for the Saviour: 'This man receiveth sinners.'

What a wonderful thing it would be, if there was joy in heaven over a sinner repenting among ourselves here on earth tonight! The word would go instantly to heaven. There's joy in the presence of the angels of God over one sinner that repenteth.

May the Lord bless his Word.

3

Believing on the Son of God

JOHN 9:35-38

Jesus heard that they had cast him out; and when he had found him, he said unto him, Dost thou believe on the Son of God? He answered and said, Who is he, Lord, that I might believe on him? And Jesus said unto him, Thou hast both seen him, and it is he that talketh with thee. And he said, Lord, I believe. And he worshipped him.

LORD'S DAY EVENING, 21ST MARCH 2004

We understand that the miracles of Jesus were performed in order to draw attention to the fact that the promised Messiah had at last come to earth. He had come, who had been promised as the one who would bring salvation to sinners. His coming was testified to by the fact that he was able to do works which no man could do.

The miracles were miracles of mercy. You'll notice that there wasn't one miracle of judgment performed on a human being during the ministry of Christ. He cursed the fig tree, and that was symbolic of the judgments that were going to come on those who rejected the Saviour, but all his miracles were miracles of mercy.

Sometimes people ask the question, 'Was it the case that those who experienced miraculous healings also experienced the saving grace of Christ?' Well, I'm not sure that there is sufficient evidence to state categorically that that was so. But certainly, the miracles of healing were illustrating what Christ had come to do in the spiritual realm, and Christ intended that his miracles would make people think about their spiritual needs and seek the supply of their spiritual needs from him.

You remember how that's brought out, for example, after the feeding of the five thousand. The Lord Jesus said to those who came after him then that they were following him, not because of the miracles, but because they had eaten of the loaves and were filled. They were not to labour for the meat that perishes, but for that meat which endureth unto life eternal, which the Son of man would give unto them, for him had God the Father sealed (John 6:26-27)—that is, he had set him apart for that purpose. So the Lord was setting down the principle there, that if you really understood the meaning of the miracles, you would seek the spiritual blessing which is illustrated by the temporal blessing.

Certainly the miracles of Christ were intended to make people think about their spiritual needs and make them realise that the one who could meet these needs was now among them. He brings that out at the beginning of this chapter when he says that the very purpose for which he came into the world was to be the light of the world. I believe that in the case of this particular man, the healing that he received when he was given his sight was illustrating the power of Christ to give spiritual sight to sinners. And indeed we have every reason to believe that the outward miracle had a spiritual parallel in this man's personal experience. Much more wonderful than the physical sight he was given was the spiritual sight, the spiritual perception, faith's view of Jesus Christ. When we look at this miracle, we are looking not just at a miracle of healing in the physical realm, but we are looking at God's work in bringing a sinner who did not know Christ to know him—a sinner who had no knowledge of the Saviour to come to believe in him and to worship him.

1. So, as the Lord might enable us, let us consider first of all this most important question that the Lord put to the man. 'When he found him, he said to him, *Dost thou believe on the Son of God?* That is a most important question. It is, perhaps we could say, *the* most important question that any person in this world can face. Dost thou believe on the Son of God?

2. And then we might consider the honest and wise response which this man gave to that question. 'He answered and said, *Who is*

he, Lord, that I might believe on him? He didn't say, 'Oh yes, I believe,' he said, 'Who is he, Lord, that I might believe on him?'

3. And then in the third place we might notice the gracious and the effective revelation which the Lord made to the man. 'He said unto him, *Thou hast both seen him, and it is he that talketh with thee.*' The Lord was giving him a gracious and an effective revelation of himself.

4. And then finally, we may notice the result—the inevitable and desirable result of that revelation. '*He said, Lord, I believe, and he worshipped him.*'

1. The Lord's question

Here is a most important question. Jesus heard that they had cast him out, and when he had found him, he said unto him, 'Dost thou believe on the Son of God?'

Now the person who asked the question was full of grace and truth, and he had been dealing very graciously with this man. Jesus came into the world in order to save sinners. He had taken notice of this man. The man didn't ask for his help. The man probably didn't know he was there and didn't know who he was, but the Lord Jesus had him in his mind from all eternity. The man's condition was in order that the glory of God would be manifested in his salvation, and Jesus dealt very graciously with him. He restored his sight—and what is more important, he raised questions in the man's mind about the identity of Christ. These questions wouldn't go away and he led him by his Spirit into clearer and clearer views of who Jesus was. Grace characterises the Lord Jesus in his dealings with this man, and in his dealings with sinners for whom he has a purpose of mercy.

Yet, although he was so gracious, and indeed *because* he was so gracious, he confronted the man with this searching question, 'Dost thou believe on the Son of God?' The Lord Jesus Christ is the one who is raising the question, the one who is bringing home to him his ignorance, the one who is requiring him to give an answer.

The man who was asked the question had experienced the Lord's goodness and he had confessed the Lord's goodness. He had spoken well of Christ, he had stood by Christ when his own parents weren't prepared to acknowledge who had done this miracle. He stood up for Christ when the enemies of Christ were treating him in a hostile manner, and at last they excommunicated him. That's what's involved in 'casting him out'—not just that they threw him out the door, but they excommunicated him from membership of the synagogue. That was a very serious matter, with social consequences. The man had experienced the Lord's goodness, he had confessed what the Lord had done for him, he had stood by the Lord, he had suffered for his acknowledgement of what Christ had done. And yet Christ puts to him the question, 'Dost thou believe on the Son of God?' You have experienced these good things in providence, you've made these confessions concerning what you knew of Christ, you've been prepared to stand up for him against his enemies, but you still have to face the question, Dost thou believe on the Son of God?

That reminds us of, for example, what the Lord Jesus said in the sermon on the mount (Matthew 7:21-23). He said, 'Many will say to me in that day, Lord, Lord.' But, Jesus said, 'Not every one that saith unto me, Lord, Lord, shall enter into the kingdom of heaven; but he that doeth the will of my Father which is in heaven. Many will say to me in that day, Lord, Lord, have we not prophesied in thy name? and in thy name have cast out devils? and in thy name done many wonderful works? And then will I profess unto them, I never knew you: depart from me, ye that work iniquity.'

It reminds us also of what the apostle Paul was saying when he was writing to the Corinthians, and emphasising the necessity of grace, the necessity of real heart religion. In chapter 13 of the first Epistle to the Corinthians he says, 'Though I speak with the tongues of men and of angels, and have not charity, I am become as sounding brass, or a tinkling cymbal. And though I have the gift of prophecy, and understand all mysteries, and all knowledge; and though I have all faith, so that I could remove mountains, and have not charity, I am nothing. And though I bestow all my goods to feed the poor, and though I give my body to be burned, and have not charity, it profiteth me nothing.'

You see, the Lord is saying to a person who has suffered for his sake, 'Dost thou believe on the Son of God? Do you *have* faith? Do you have real religion?' The Lord is saying to a person who's preached the gospel all his days, 'Dost *thou* believe on the Son of God? Do you have personal saving faith in Christ?' Whatever we've done, whatever we've suffered, whatever we've said, however much we've stood by Christ when everyone else was against him, we still have to face the question—the Lord still puts the question to us— 'Dost thou believe on the Son of God?' You'll not get to heaven by wonderful experiences in providence. You'll not get to heaven by speaking well for Christ among his enemies. You'll not get to heaven by suffering for his sake, or even by being a martyr for the sake of Jesus. Dost thou believe on the Son of God? That's the question that this questioner puts to this man.

And what an important question! It's a question regarding our view of Christ. When he was asked who had healed him, this man said, 'A man called Jesus.' And as they went on interrogating him, he said, 'He's a prophet.' And then he said, 'He has come from God.' But has he seen the glory of the person of the Saviour? Not just a man—not just a prophet—not just of divine origin—but the Son of God in our nature, God manifest in the flesh? The Lord is asking this man, and he's asking us, 'What really is your view of Christ? Are you seeing him in all his glory as the God-man Redeemer? Are you realising that the Saviour you need cannot be less than God—that you need a Redeemer who is able to do what only God can do?' What is our own view of Christ?

And he's asking him about his own faith in that Redeemer. Not only, 'Do you know the truth about him? Are you well aware of the fact that God was manifest in the flesh? That this person is God and man in two distinct natures and one person for ever?' You know that truth, you believe that truth, as far as you can understand yourself. You don't feel any inclination to question that God was manifest in the flesh. But the question the Lord is putting is, 'Dost thou *believe* on the Son of God?' Do you believe on him? Are you resting in him? Have you entrusted yourself to him as your own Saviour?

And then he's making it very personal. He says, 'Dost *thou* believe?' In fact, 'thou' is the first word in the sentence. Literally it says 'thou believest in the Son of God,' and then there is a question mark at the end. As we would say nowadays, 'You do believe in the Son of God, don't you?' That's the way it's being put. But it's being put very personally. 'Whom do men say that I am?' No doubt it's very interesting to know all the different views that people hold concerning Christ, and to be able to repudiate them. But the question is put to us, 'What does he mean to yourself?' Whom say *ye* that I am?

That's the kind of question we are confronted with here. Whoever we are, whatever we've done, whatever we've said, whatever we've experienced, the Lord is setting himself before us in his glory as the Son of God, as the only Redeemer of God's elect, and he is asking us if we *believe* on him. Do we really trust in him? And do we trust in him *ourselves*? Whatever others think about him, is that what he means to us personally?

That's a very important question, because everything depends on it. As John's Gospel said earlier, 'For God so loved the world, that he gave his only begotten Son, that whosoever *believeth* in him should not perish, but have everlasting life' (John 3:16). And as that same chapter concludes, it's those who believe on the Son of God who have everlasting life. Those who do not believe the Son of God shall not see life, but the wrath of God abideth on them (John 3:36). No question could be more important or more urgent, than that.

2. The man's honest and wise response

Well then, notice the honest response and the wise response that this man gave to the Lord's question. He answered and said, 'Who is he, Lord, that I might believe on him?' He is not being rushed into a profession of faith. He's not going to profess a faith he does not have. But notice that he's not asking, 'What does it mean to believe on him?' or, 'How can I believe in him?'

You see, sometimes that's the way we put our question when we're confronted with this question from the Lord. There are people who have been followed by that question everywhere they've gone, over a period of time, when they get up in the morning, when they go to bed at night. Whatever they do, when there's a moment of reflection, what comes into their minds is this: 'Do I have faith in Christ? Dost thou believe on the Son of God? Is Christ a Saviour to me?' And sometimes the response is, 'Oh, if I only knew what it means to believe in him! And if I only *could* believe in him—if only I knew *how* to believe in him!' These are of course legitimate questions in their own place. What does it mean to believe in him? How *can* I believe in him?

But you see, this man didn't come up with these questions. These were not the questions that surfaced in his soul at this time. His question was, 'Who is he, Lord, that I might believe on him?' How can I believe in him when I don't know him? How can I believe in one of whom I am ignorant? If he was revealed to me, if he became known to me, then I could believe in him.

You see, he was realising—he was being taught by the Holy Spirit—that if he was going to believe in Christ, then Christ would have to make himself known to him. How can they believe in him of whom they have not heard? How they can believe in him of whom they know nothing? There's no use just bringing up the name of Jesus and saying, 'Believe in Jesus and you'll be saved!' 'But who is he, Lord?'

This is a *confession of ignorance* on his part. We ought to be ashamed of our ignorance but (as 'Rabbi' Duncan said) we should not be ashamed to confess our ignorance to the Lord. That is what this man is doing, and he's a very good example of the way that grace teaches people. We should be ashamed of our ignorance. The Bible is clear enough. The revelation that is given of Christ in the pages of Scripture is clear enough. It's written in language that anyone who can read can understand. And even those who cannot yet read, they can understand when it's read to them—they can understand it as far as forming mental notions of the matter is concerned. The reason we don't *know* him when he reveals himself in his Word is to be found in the ignorance of our own hearts, the blindness of our own minds toward the Saviour—'the natural man receiveth not the things of the

Spirit of God' (1 Corinthians 2:14). We have to be ashamed of that ignorance, because it is sinful ignorance. But we shouldn't be ashamed to confess it. We shouldn't be afraid to confess it to the Lord. The Lord delights when a poor sinner is constrained to confess his ignorance as this man did. Who is he, Lord?

But not only is he confessing his ignorance, he's expressing *a genuine desire to come to know him*. He wants to know Christ, the Son of God. And he wants to believe in him. That's the way the grace of God works in the souls of sinners—it convicts them of their ignorance of Christ and of their unbelief, and then gives them a real, living and earnest desire to come to know the Saviour. 'O that I knew him—that he would become the object of my faith! There's nothing I want more,' the soul is saying, 'than to have that acquaintance with Christ which will persuade me and enable me to receive him and to rest on him as my Saviour.' That's in this man's response. He's desiring the knowledge of Christ, and he's desiring to be able to believe on the Lord Jesus Christ.

And another thing that's in his response is this: *he's applying to the Lord himself* to make himself known to him. He's confessing his ignorance, he's expressing his desire to know the Lord, and he's asking the Lord to make himself known. 'Who is he, Lord, that I might believe on him?' He's saying in effect what Hector MacPhail taught the Highland kitchen maid to say. As MacPhail was travelling south he met her, and he got her to promise to pray, 'Lord, show me myself.' Show me *myself*! She was in a terrible state when he came back, because she had got a view of herself as a sinner. And he said that now she was to pray, 'Lord, show me *thyself*.' And that is what this man in effect is praying. 'Lord, who is he? Show me him! Show me thyself—make thyself known to me!'

That's a wise and honest response on the part of any sinner who has been convicted of his ignorance, and who has been given a concern to know the Lord and to believe in the Lord. Oh that the Lord himself would make himself known to me, that he would reveal himself to me, in a way that would constrain me and compel me, to believe in him! Who is he, Lord, that I might believe on him, in order that I might believe on him. Is there anything of that response in our own souls? A person might be saying, 'Well, I feel so ignorant of him, and I feel so unable to believe in him, but oh that the Lord himself would teach me, that he would enlighten me. It's not enough to have the light shining around me—I need to have the spiritual vision whereby I can see Christ.' You see, Christ is in the gospel very clearly. Very clearly! But are we seeing him with the eye of faith? We know *about* him—we know much more about him than this man ever knew in this world. But is it our concern to be able to say with the apostle, 'I know *whom* I have believed,' to have a personal believing knowledge of the Saviour?

3. The gracious and the effective revelation which Christ made of himself to the man

Well, we find the Lord revealing himself graciously and effectively to this man. The man confessed his ignorance. He expressed his earnest desire to know and to believe in Christ. He applied for the Lord to make Christ known to his soul. And the Lord's gracious response was, 'Thou hast both seen him, and it is he that talketh with thee.' In other words, 'I am he.'

This reminds us very much of the experience of the woman of Samaria—how the Lord brought her gradually to a sense of her sinfulness and to a desire for Christ. We believe that that's what she had when she said, 'When Christ cometh, he will tell us all things.' She was feeling so ignorant, and she was feeling so much in need of Christ, and then he said to her, 'I that speak unto thee am he.'

It's similar with this man. The Lord has brought him along a way that must have been perplexing to him at the time. The Lord used his providence, but he was also working in him by his Spirit. The man was trying to understand his experiences, he was trying to understand the person who had dealt so kindly with him—he's a man called Jesus, he's a prophet, he's not a sinner, he cannot be a sinner, he's a man who has come from God. You can see how his mind is working on the subject, how he is being brought to clearer views of Christ. But he's been brought to the place too where he has to acknowledge,

'I'll never know the truth unless the Lord will make the truth known to me.' And here is the Lord responding, graciously, by revealing himself to him.

It wasn't enough for the man to reflect on his experiences. It wasn't enough for the man to try to work things out in his own mind. He had to do that—and we have to do that too. We have to reflect on what God has done for us and in us. We have to try to reckon with the truth as far as we understand it—we have to try to come to an understanding of Christ and the way of salvation. But when it comes to the bit, we have to acknowledge that, because of our own sinfulness and perversity, we need something even beyond the written Word—we need the Holy Spirit to enlighten our minds in the knowledge of Christ. We need Christ in the Scriptures to reveal himself to us. It's only in the Scriptures Christ *is* revealed. We mustn't expect to have a revelation of Christ apart from the Scriptures. Perhaps some of us, some of the time, almost treat the Scriptures as if they are not sufficient, and as if we need something other than the Scriptures to make Christ known to us. But the Scriptures *are* sufficient. The Scriptures constitute the one revelation of Christ that we will ever have in this world. But still, you see, what we need is that the power of the Spirit of God will accompany the revelation of Christ that's in the Bible, so that we'll be able to perceive it—so that we'll be able to take it in, we'll be able to understand it, we'll be able to recognise him, and be able to trust in him as our Lord and our God.

That is what Christ did for this man. He said, 'Thou hast both seen him, and it is he that talketh with thee.' 'I am he.' The very fact that the man could see Christ at all was a wonder, and it reminded him of all that the Lord had done for him. But, you see, he needed to be given this conviction by the Lord himself. The Lord's word carried conviction, it carried power, *with it*. That's what you need and what I need, in order that Christ would become Christ *to us*—in order that we might be enabled to receive him for what he is. We need the power of the Holy Spirit, the power of Christ through his Holy Spirit, to accompany this word. John the Baptist said, 'Behold the Lamb of God!' That's what the gospel is saying to us. That's what Christ is saying to us in his Word. He's setting himself before us. This is the only Saviour. This is the only Redeemer. How suitable he is! How clear the revelation is! It's a revelation which is sufficient to oblige us to believe—to warrant us to believe—to make our unbelief a sin. The revelation of Christ in the Bible is a revelation that is sufficient ground for any sinner to come to know Christ and to believe in Christ. It's the only warrant we'll ever have, the warrant of his Word, of his gospel. But the problem is with us. The problem is in the darkness of our own minds, the enmity of our own mind against God, against Christ. The god of this world has blinded the minds of those who believe not, lest the light of the glorious gospel of Christ would shine in. It's a combination of our own darkness and the devil's darkening of our minds which means that we need what the apostle spoke of: 'God, who commanded the light to shine out of darkness, hath shined in our hearts, to give the light of the knowledge of the glory of God in the face of Jesus Christ' (2 Corinthians 4:6). We need the one who said 'I am the light of the world' to shine in our hearts, to give us the vision, to give us the sight, the spiritual perception, that will enable us to rest on the Saviour.

This is something that is emphasised so much in the Bible. You remember how we have it at the beginning of this Gospel. Christ is spoken of there as the light that came into the world. But 'he was in the world, and the world was made by him, and the world knew him not. He came unto his own, and his own received him not. But as many as received him, to them gave he power to become the sons of God, even to them that believe on his name: which were born, not of blood, nor of the will of the flesh, nor of the will of man, but of God. And the Word was made flesh, and dwelt among us, (and we beheld his glory, the glory as of the only begotten of the Father,) full of grace and truth.' (John 1:10-14). Christ is light—he has brought the light of salvation into this world—but in order to behold it, in order to receive it, we need a supernatural work of grace. We need to be born of God, we need to be enlightened by the Holy Spirit, we need this spiritual capacity which we don't have by nature. That's what Christ was giving this man, when he said, 'Thou hast both seen him, and it is he that talketh with thee.' He's making himself known as the Christ of God—a most gracious revelation—a revelation which we need, not because the Word of God is deficient, but because of the perversity of our own nature.

4. The inevitable and desirable result of Christ's revelation of himself

Well then, we see the result of this—the inevitable result, the desirable result—of Christ revealing himself to a soul. 'He said, Lord, I believe, and he worshipped him.'

If a person is shown the glory of Christ as a Saviour by Christ himself, that person can't help believing in him. Our problem is, 'How can I believe? What does it mean to believe?' But, you see, that problem disappears when the soul becomes acquainted with the glory of Christ as a Saviour, because that revelation of Christ has the power to constrain faith in the soul of the sinner. When you look at the Lord's people and their experience, you will find that they don't say, 'I studied the Bible and I studied what faith was, and I decided I was going to believe in Christ, and I believed in him, and I was saved.' But what happens is this—whatever struggles they had with unbelief and their inability to believe, when Christ made himself known to them by the gracious power of his Spirit, there was nothing else they could do but trust in him. There was nothing else they could do but rely on him to save them from their sins. Maybe they didn't know what they were doing. Maybe they were still wondering, 'Do I believe in him?' Faith coming into existence, and the consciousness that one has faith, are not always together, as far as the sequence of things is concerned. Often they are, often they're not. But the point is, whatever is the case with regard to our consciousness of the matter, when a person gets a glimpse of Christ as a Saviour by the work of God's Spirit in the soul, that person cannot help trusting in him. From that time forth, Christ becomes the only ground of confidence that person has. In some, they may be saying, 'Who can tell?' In others, they may be able to say, 'I know whom I have believed.' But wherever Christ is made known, by the power of his Spirit, to a soul that is seeking him, that soul believes. 'He said, Lord, I believe.'

That's the effect of divine revelation. The man could have gone on reasoning all his days, 'Who is this person, who healed me so miraculously?' He could have heard Christ preaching, as many did. He could have heard the disciples preaching. He could have read the Bible if he lived long enough for the New Testament to be written. He could read everything we've ever read and hear everything we've ever heard. But because of his corruption, he would never have come to say, 'Lord, I believe,' if the Lord had not made himself known. But when the Lord made himself known—when the Lord said, 'It is I—thou hast both seen him and it is he that talketh with thee'—then the man said, 'Lord, I believe.' Faith was born in his soul.

And how do we know that it wasn't just an empty profession? 'He worshipped him.' That's what showed that he believed that Jesus was the Son of God. A person might say, 'I believe Jesus is the Son of God,' but if they continue to treat him as a mere man, that shows that their faith is not genuine. But when a person does believe that Jesus is the Son of God, that person treats Jesus as the Son of God, and that person worships him. That person honours him, adores him, regards him as God, worships him as he worships the Father, and worships him as he worships the Holy Spirit. He worships Jesus by trusting him, by loving him, by obeying him, by seeking to follow him wherever he leads him. Worship is a very comprehensive thing—it's honouring him, honouring him for what he is. And how can one honour Christ better than by trusting in him?

'He said, I believe, and he worshipped him.' This reminds us of Moses' experience. Moses prayed to God, 'Show me thy glory' (Exodus 33:18). The Lord had said he was going to go with the Israelites, but Moses felt he needed to know the God who was going with him—he needed to know something of his glory. He prayed there in Exodus 33, 'Show me thy glory.' Then we have the Lord responding to that prayer which he had put in Moses' heart. 'And the Lord descended in the cloud, and stood with him there, and proclaimed the name of the Lord. And the Lord passed by before him, and proclaimed, The Lord, the Lord God, merciful and gracious, longsuffering, and abundant in goodness and truth, keeping mercy for thousands, forgiving iniquity and transgression and sin, and that will by no means clear the guilty; visiting the iniquity of the fathers upon the children, and upon the children's children, unto the third and to the fourth generation.' (Exodus 34:5-7). God was making himself known—graciously, powerfully—to Moses. And what was the effect? 'Moses made haste, and bowed his head toward the earth, and worshipped.'

That has always been the effect when God has made himself known to a sinner in Christ. That sinner has become a worshipper—a worshipper of the Father, and a worshipper of the Son, and a worshipper of the Holy Ghost. That's the best evidence of faith a person can have. To you who believe, he is precious (1 Peter 2:7). To you who believe, he has become the object of worship. You adore him, you honour him, you wish to follow him and to be with him and to glorify him in time and in eternity. Well, that didn't come out of your fallen human nature. That came out of faith's view of Christ.

When we think of the Lord's dealings with this man, we may notice that we should be thankful to the Lord even for the most difficult providences which may be in our experience, if these are the means of bringing Christ and ourselves together. That's how it must have been with this man. I'm sure he must have been thankful even for those years he spent in blindness, when he thought that, if it wasn't for being in that condition, the Lord would never have taken any notice of him. The providences we pass through may be dark and they may be difficult, but what a mercy if they are the means of bringing us to the attention of the Saviour, and bringing the Saviour to our aid.

Also, we see here that in all our perplexities and difficulties and questions concerning ourselves and concerning Christ, we should be seeking to be brought at last to the place where we will desire the Lord to enlighten us in the matter. Why does the Lord bring people through the perplexing experiences such as those through which this man passed? So that he'll bring them to the place where they are ready to be taught by God's grace. They've tried to understand as best they can by themselves, they've done what they could, and they realise that they're utterly dependent on the Lord to make himself known to them in his grace. That's what happened to this man. He went through all these experiences. It must have been extremely trying for him—on a day when you'd think everyone would be so happy at what had happened to him, instead he was put through these most gruelling experiences and his mind was so filled with anxieties and concerns and uncertainties. Was it not just to prepare him to confess his ignorance, when the question was put to him, 'Dost thou believe in the Son of God?' and to prepare him to apply to the Lord to give him light on the matter, to make himself known to him as the Saviour. All these perplexities are not in vain, if they bring us to the place where we say, 'Who is he, Lord, that I might believe on him?'

And also, how thankful we should be for the revelation which the Lord has made to his people of himself—the revelation he has given in the pages of his Word, and the revelation that he has applied to the soul by the power of his Holy Spirit. That's where faith is created, and that's where faith is sustained. God's people have to be continually praying the same prayer, that the Lord would show them himself, because that's what creates faith, what constrains faith in the soul, and what keeps it in existence.

Finally, if God has given us that faith in Christ, then what else can we do but worship him? What reasons we have for praising God for Jesus Christ! What reasons we have for praising Christ for all that he is, and for all that he has done, for our salvation! 'I believe,' he said, 'and he worshipped him.' That's really the intended outcome of all that the Lord does in the experience of his people. That's why worship is *the* function of the church—it doesn't exist for other functions, but for the worship of God. That's why sinners are converted, that's why saints are edified—that God will get the glory that is due to his name. That, I believe, is what is close to the hearts of those who do believe, although they feel so little of the spirit of worship. This *is* their concern, this *is* their desire, and that's why they're looking forward, by the grace of God, to a world in which they will be able to worship him perfectly.

May the Lord bless his Word.

4

Themes in 1 John
God's revelation in Scripture

1 JOHN 1:1-4

That which was from the beginning, which we have heard, which we have seen with our eyes, which we have looked upon, and our hands have handled, of the Word of life; (for the life was manifested, and we have seen it, and bear witness, and shew unto you that eternal life, which was with the Father, and was manifested unto us;) that which we have seen and heard declare we unto you, that ye also may have fellowship with us: and truly our fellowship is with the Father, and with his Son Jesus Christ. And these things write we unto you, that your joy may be full.

LORD'S DAY MORNING, 30TH MARCH 2008

In these words, the apostle John is explaining the reason for his writing this Epistle, and perhaps also the reason for his writing the Gospel, and the reason for Scripture in general. We are dependent on Scripture for the doctrines that we believe, the faith we have, the experience we have, and the way of life that we live.

Our Shorter Catechism tells us that the Word of God, which is contained in the Scriptures of the Old and New Testaments, is the only rule to direct us how we may glorify and enjoy God. And one might just say in passing, when it says 'contained in the Scriptures' it doesn't mean (as people try to make out nowadays) that the Word of God is within the Bible and other things are within the Bible too. The word 'contained' is used in a sense which is quite common with ourselves, and that is, it is confined to it, it is restricted within it. We speak about a fire being contained or water being contained or enemy forces being contained. What is meant is that they are confined to a certain area. And the Word of God which we have is contained in the Scriptures, you cannot find it anywhere else. All Scripture is the Word of God. And as the Catechism also tells us, the Scriptures teach us what we are to believe concerning God. They also teach us how we are to live in this world, and they are the basis of our religion—the infallible and unerring Scriptures.

Here the apostle John is concentrating attention on the particular function of Scripture in enabling us to share with the original disciples of Christ the knowledge which they have of him, and the fellowship which they had with him, and the joy which is the consequence of that fellowship. The Bible enables us to know Christ just as well as John knew him, and to enter into fellowship with God and to enter into fellowship with Christ, just as John did. That's a tremendous thing. There's not a word in the Bible about the physical appearance of Christ—that's not the kind of knowledge that matters. We don't know him after the flesh any more, the apostle Paul said (2 Corinthians 5:16). Knowing Christ is not knowing what he looked like, but knowing Christ is knowing him for the person that he is. And that knowledge is as available to you and to me as it was to those who lived with him, who walked with him, who heard him, who saw him, who touched him, when he was here in this world in our nature.

In the light of these verses I would like to try to say a little about three things, as the Lord may enable me.

1. First of all, the nature of Scripture—what does John tell us about the nature of Scripture, the nature of what is written in the Bible?

2. And secondly, the content of Scripture—what is the subject matter of the writings which we have in the Bible?

3. And then, thirdly, the purpose of Scripture—why has Scripture been given to us?

1. The nature of Scripture

Well, first of all, we learn something about the nature of Scripture. We are not dependent on these verses alone for that. Elsewhere we are told very distinctly, for example by the apostle Paul writing to Timothy, that the Scriptures which are able to make us wise unto salvation through faith in Christ are given by inspiration of God, they are breathed out by God (2 Timothy 3:15-16). As Peter says, the writers were not giving the fruits of their own researches, but holy men of God spake as they were moved by the Holy Ghost (2 Peter 1:21). God prepared these people: he gave them their mind, he gave them their characteristics, he gave them their particular talents, and these shined through in the different writings. Once you know a little about John and Peter and Paul, you can discern the different natural characteristics of these men and their writings. They had these because God was preparing them for the work that they had to do. And then he gave them the thoughts, the gracious thoughts he had were revealed to them. And he gave them the words. They were their own words at one level but they are also the words of God, because God was ensuring that they would express his thoughts in the words that were most in keeping with his mind and that most clearly revealed what he had to say. So that's the general picture of the nature of Scripture that is given to us in the Bible, that it is not the word of man, it's the Word of God, and it's the Word of God because God made sure that they communicated exactly what he wanted us to know. So when we read the words of John and Peter and Paul and the others—yes, they wrote them, but they were moved by the Holy Ghost, and there is not one word that they uttered that could have been put better. There is not one error in the statements of the Bible: there is not one error in the doctrines and the thoughts, there is not one error in the words which they used, because God was in control of them.

But John uses two words which bring before us certain aspects of the nature of Scripture. He says first that we *bear witness*: 'We have seen it and bear witness' (verse 2), and then he says, 'that which we have seen and heard *declare* we unto you' (verse 3). The writers of

WITH AN EVERLASTING LOVE

Scripture are bearing witness: they are witness-bearers, they are eyewitnesses, they are telling what God has said, what God has done, what they have seen, what they have heard, what they have touched. The apostle uses all these words. He is writing as someone who saw Christ and who heard him and who touched him. He is giving testimony to facts of which he himself is personally aware, and he is speaking as a credible witness and with the authority of a credible witness.

And that is true with regard to all the writers of Scripture: they are bearing accurate testimony of what they saw and heard of God. And that is something that honest critics cannot challenge—the integrity of the writers of Scripture. They are telling what they know, they are telling what they have seen, they are telling it as it really is, they are credible witnesses of the truth as it is in Jesus. And an honest man's report is something that one can rely on. If a person has a character for honesty then one can go by the testimony that that person bears to some fact or other.

But John also speaks, he says, in the sense of *declaring* what he has seen and heard (verse 3). That word refers to a report from someone, a report which one has been commissioned to declare to others. We are not depending just on the experience of an honest man, we are depending on the word of a person who was given that word to speak by God. That is a much greater ground of confidence, because we might say, 'Well, he is an honest man, but he could have been mistaken.' But this honest man is not mistaken, because what he is communicating is not just the testimony of his own experience, but also the message that God has given to him. He is declaring the Word of God, he is an ambassador, he is a representative. He's not making it up himself, he's not reflecting on his own experience of Christ. He's communicating a message which he has been given by God. He said, 'We have seen it and we bear witness, and show unto you that eternal life which was with the Father and was manifested unto us— that which we have seen and heard declare we unto you.' There is the authority of personal experience, but also and especially, the authority of a commissioned messenger.

Wasn't that what the psalmist said when he was on his death bed? He said many precious things, but in particular he said, 'The Spirit of the Lord spake by me, and his word was in my tongue' (2 Samuel 23:2). That's what John is saying. This is the testimony of an honest witness, but it's also the message of a commissioned representative, a commissioned ambassador, who cannot tamper with the message, but who is declaring and speaking from God to men.

How thankful we should be that we have a book of which these things can be said. This is the inspired Word of God—the testimony of credible witnesses, yes, but also the testimony of the infallible God. Surely we can rely on that. No wonder the psalmist could say that he found a sure ground for his hope in the Word of God.

2. The content of Scripture

The second thing we might just notice is the content of Scripture. Of course Scripture contains references and teaching concerning many subjects, particularly relating to religion and morals, but also covering a wide area of human life and existence. Everything that is necessary to be known by us in order that we could be saved and in order that we can glorify God is communicated to us in the Bible.

But particularly the Bible focuses upon Christ. Christ is the content of the Bible. Christ is the message of the Scriptures from the book of Genesis through to the book of Revelation. He taught his own disciples that. Especially after his resurrection he drew their attention to that. The law, the prophets, the psalms—they all spoke of him, they all led to him. Christ may be much more evident in some Scriptures than in others, but every Scripture leads one to Christ in one way or another.

That is the beauty of Scripture, the harmony of Scripture—what gives it its beauty and harmony is the centrality of the Lord Jesus Christ in all the Scriptures. He was able to speak about the things concerning himself (Luke 24:27). Some parts of the Bible, taken on their own, we might find it more difficult to see Christ in—when you read the genealogies and some of the historical accounts perhaps—

but when you look at them in the wider picture, they are all telling part of the process whereby Christ was coming into the world and whereby God was accomplishing his purposes which are centred on the Saviour. Abraham saw his day, Isaiah spoke of him when he saw his glory, the prophets were searching what the Spirit of Christ who was in them signified, when he spoke beforehand of the sufferings of Christ, and the glory that should follow (1 Peter 1:11). As I've mentioned before, there was a common saying in the past, 'every little path eventually leads to London.' So every part of Scripture leads to Christ, although of course Christ is made very clear particularly in the Scriptures of the New Testament.

Well, Christ is the theme of the Scriptures, and Christ is the theme to which John is drawing our attention here. The core description of him, we believe, in these verses is *the Word of life*. He says, 'We have heard, we have seen with our eyes, we have looked upon, our hands have handled, of *the Word of life*' (verse 1). Our translators have put a capital at the beginning of 'Word' because they obviously believed it referred to Christ. And that is quite in keeping with what John said at the beginning of his Gospel, when he spoke about *the Word*. 'In the beginning was the Word, and the Word was with God, and the Word was God' (John 1:1). He uses somewhat different terminology, or he uses the terminology in a different way in this passage, but he is referring to the same person, the Word of life.

This expression refers to the life manifested, the life come to expression, the life in action, the life being communicated to others. God is life. The Bible doesn't use that precise terminology—it says 'God is light' and 'God is love'—but it uses terms which come to the same thing. It speaks about the living God, the God who has life in himself, emphasising the self-existence of God, emphasising the life and activity of God, emphasising the life-giving power of God—all life is derived from him. And Jesus Christ is the image of the invisible God (Colossians 1:15). He is identical in his essence with the Father, and in his human nature he is the manifestation of God, he is the revelation of God, he has life in himself. He has the divine qualities, the divine powers. And John is speaking about him, therefore, as

God manifest, the Word of life, the revelation of the eternal life which God is.

You notice that John says various things about this person, the Word of life. He was *from the beginning*. It doesn't matter how far back you go, it doesn't matter what beginning you think of: he was there, he was in the beginning with God, he has eternal existence. He is the same yesterday, today and for ever (Hebrews 13:8). You can never get back to a beginning where he is not. What a way to emphasise the fact that this person about whom he is speaking is God, eternal God!

And he speaks about him also as *having been manifested*, so that 'we have heard him speaking, we have seen him with our eyes, we have looked upon him.' And that word 'looked on' is emphasising more than seeing: it means we have penetrated into the reality of him. We might think 'we have looked upon him' just as an outward glance—but no, we have seen him with our eyes and looked upon him, we have investigated, we have seen him at close quarters, we have come to know the truth concerning him.

And 'our hands have handled him.' John's head was on his bosom. How often they must have made contact with each other! He is God manifest in the flesh, he is the one living and true God, he was with the Father and he has been manifested unto us. God manifest in the flesh. What a great mystery that is! This one person is God and man, two distinct natures, one person for ever. It is beyond the power of our mind to comprehend—a person who is God, who has all the qualities of God, the infinity of God, the eternity of God, the unchangeableness of God, and yet he has a nature which began to be, he has human nature, limited, finite, begun in time, subject to all manner of weaknesses.

And this is the manifestation of *life eternal*. This is the manifestation of God, God in our nature. Of course the whole purpose of that was that he might save his people from their sins.

The content of Scripture is Christ. We preach Christ crucified, the Son of God, Jesus Christ. *His Son Jesus Christ*—that's bringing it together again. This is the theme that John was concentrating upon, as he was led to do so by the Spirit in his Gospel—that ye might believe that Jesus Christ is the Son of God—and in his Epistle too—

that he has come in the flesh, that this is the Son of God with power—and yet he is Jesus, born of Mary to be the Saviour of his people from their sins, appointed by God, anointed by God to be their Messiah, their Christ. Yes, the content of Scripture is Jesus Christ. 'Search the scriptures; for in them ye think ye have eternal life: and these are they which testify of me.' Have you found Christ—have I found Christ—in the Scriptures? Are we looking for him in the Scriptures? Can it be said of us, 'I know that ye seek Jesus, which was crucified'? This is where he is found: he is found in the pages of his Word.

3. The purpose of Scripture

That brings us to the third thing, the main point perhaps which John is making, and that is the purpose of Scripture. 'These things declare we unto you, that ye also may have fellowship with us: and truly our fellowship is with the Father, and with his Son Jesus Christ, and these things write we unto you, that your joy may be full.'

The Scriptures have been given so that sinners can come to know God and Jesus Christ whom he has sent. We are dependent on them for everything we know about God, for everything we know about Christ. We are dependent on them (when they are blessed to us by the Holy Spirit) for a personal acquaintance with the Saviour, and for fellowship with the Saviour and with God, to whom the Saviour leads his people. It is through the Scriptures, through believing, that we get life and comfort and holiness. Everything we need to know is here in order to promote spiritual life, in order to prepare us for eternity.

And the apostle is drawing attention to the fact that it is through Scripture that we can enjoy *fellowship with him*, with them, with John and with other writers. That doesn't mean that we have some sort of mystical association with the saints that have gone. The fellowship with them is sharing with them in the knowledge and fellowship that they had with Christ. We don't walk with Abraham or with Isaiah. We don't walk and talk with Abraham and Isaiah and John. But along with them we can walk and talk with Christ and with his Father.

Because the Scriptures are the means whereby the reality of Christ and the presence of Christ are communicated to us, with the same spiritual reality as they were communicated to these ancient believers. The Scriptures are the means of giving reality to Christ in the experience of the Lord's people.

That's really the point which Hugh Martin is illustrating throughout his book, *The Abiding Presence*. There are two things he speaks about—the biography of Christ, and the presence of Christ by his Spirit. 'Biography' isn't a very good word to apply to the Gospels or to the Scriptures, because they don't set out to be a biography in the normal sense, but we know what he means. There's the biography, there is the account concerning Christ. And there's the presence of Christ by his Spirit in the souls and lives of his people. And it's by means of the account—by means of the biography that we have in the Bible—that the presence of Christ, which is made real to his people by the Spirit, has real form. It's intelligible, it's understandable to them. And it's the presence of Christ by the Spirit that makes what is written in the Scriptures to be a reality to the child of God. The presence by the Spirit and the testimony given in the Scriptures *together* are what make Christ real and near and precious to his people. We cannot have the one without the other; both are necessary.

And what the apostle is bringing before us is the fact that it is through the Scriptures, through what is written by these eyewitnesses, by these commissioned, inspired servants of God, that Christ as they knew him becomes known to us. He becomes a reality to us. That's something very different from reading any human biography of an ordinary human individual. Some biographies do give a very real impression of a person's character and life, and you feel you get to know a lot about them. But you don't have communion with them, you don't trust them, you don't love them, you don't speak to them. But it's so different with the Word of God, because it's not a person of the past that is brought before us here, but one who is the same yesterday, today and for ever. And the truth concerning him is communicated in such a way by the Spirit of the Lord that he is as real to us as any other person is, and we can trust him, we can love him, we can know him, we can serve him, we can have communion with him, we can receive from him, we can speak to him. And that's what the apostle is drawing our attention to when he speaks about it, 'that you may have fellowship with us'—not that you will have some sort of mysterious connection with us, but that you'll have the same view of Christ and same experience of Christ as we had.

And so he speaks about Scripture promoting *fellowship with the Father, and with his Son Jesus Christ*. Because of the constant repetition of the benediction, we're quite used to the expression, 'the communion of the Holy Ghost'—the fellowship of the Holy Ghost. But there is a fellowship, a communion with each person of the Godhead. The Holy Ghost is the person who is the medium (as it were) of that communication. He leads us to the Father through Christ. We have fellowship with the Holy Spirit in that he is working in us and we are depending on him. But the Holy Spirit, on whose indwelling we are absolutely dependent, is very much setting the Father and Christ before us. And that is what we have here, an emphasis on fellowship with the Father and with his Son Jesus Christ. Fellowship—with the three persons of the Godhead. Communion— God communicating to us and we responding to that communication, as we are enabled by the Spirit of the Lord. That is the essence of the fellowship, the essence of the communion: the Lord God communicating to us and we responding to that communication. It's not an elation of spirit. So often nowadays this sort of thing, fellowship with the Father and with the Son, would be thought of as a very ecstatic sort of experience. But fellowship is walking with God, a habit of dependence, a habit of drawing out of his fulness. It's a way of life, a life lived in submission to the will of God, a life lived in dependence on the grace of God.

He mentions *fellowship with the Father*. The Father is the great representative of the Godhead, the source of salvation—the Father's love electing and purposing to save his people from their sins and providing Christ for them. We have fellowship with the Father. He loves us, and we love him because he first loved us (1 John 4:19). We respond to that love as we are enabled by the grace of God. We depend on that sovereign love. And he mentions *fellowship with Jesus*

Christ his Son, the Redeemer of God's elect. Receiving him, resting on him, loving him, drawing out of his fulness, and seeking to live to his praise and to his glory. These are the sorts of things that characterise fellowship with the Father and with his Son Jesus Christ. There's a coming and going between God and his people which manifests itself in this life of reliance on him and on his grace.

And that's why Scripture has been given—so that we can walk with God as Enoch did, so that we can enjoy friendship with God as Abraham did. It's not the kind of feeling that lifts people up, elevates them, makes them feel wonderful. It may sometimes make them feel very much the *opposite* of wonderful. Fellowship with the Father and with his Son Jesus Christ can be a very humbling thing, because in the light of it, we see our own sinfulness, we see how unworthy we are of having any friendly, saving relationship with God in Christ. But this fellowship is more the habit of the mind, the habit of the soul—being in harmony with God, thinking as God thinks, having the same view of things as God has, especially having the same view of Christ, the same view of sin, the same view of salvation. That's fellowship with God and with his Son Jesus Christ, when the mind that was in Christ is in us, when we are looking at things in the fear of the Lord, looking at things from the standpoint of God himself. 'That you may have fellowship with us, and truly—really what I mean is this—that you would have fellowship with the Father and with his Son Jesus Christ.'

'And these things write we unto you, *that your joy may be full*—so that you'll be full of joy, so that your joy will be increased, and you will really be able to joy in God through our Lord Jesus Christ, by whom we have now received the atonement. The Christian life is a joyful life, and it will be all the more joyful in proportion as we are more and more acquainted with Christ in the Scriptures, and the more we are enabled to enter with John and others into this fellowship with the Father and with his Son. It's not a flippant life. It's not the kind of life that is characterised by the joy that so many associate with evangelical religion—singing songs and playing music and living jauntily. That's just the joy of the world with a religious coating. I'm afraid there is so much religion—and we have to beware of it ourselves—that is just a religious sugar put on the pill of worldliness and sin. One can go to hell full of religion, full of the joys of religion, if one is thinking of religion and joy in that sort of way. But the joy that is spoken of here is the satisfaction of the soul with God, and the satisfaction which comes from knowing that one is accepted in Christ, that one has an interest in God and in his salvation. We joy in God.

We also joy as a consequence of knowing that God has loved us and that Christ is our Saviour. And John's Gospel and John's Epistles, particularly the First Epistle, were intended to strengthen the assurance of the Lord's people so that they could enjoy their fellowship with God, so that they could enjoy their relationship with God. This is a joy which survives even the greatest trials of faith in this world. That's the wonderful thing about the joy of the Lord's people. You can see it at times in some of them, when the Lord has tried their faith greatly and they can't go around pretending that they're bright and breezy. But they still have a soul's satisfaction with God. They are satisfied with him, they are satisfied with his will, they believe there is nobody more blessed on the face of the earth than the people of God. 'Happy art thou, O Israel: who is like unto thee, O people saved by the Lord' (Deuteronomy 33:29).

'These things,' he says, 'we have written unto you, that your joy may be full'—so that you'd be as full of joy as it is possible to be in this world. We know that joy in all its fulness is something that will be experienced in heaven. We were trying to look at that recently: 'In thy presence is fulness of joy' (Psalm 16:11). When we see him as he is, when we are in the immediate presence of the Saviour, when we have been delivered from sin, the presence of it, the power of it, the love of it, delivered from temptation, delivered from all the consequences of sin in this world—then our joy will be full and nothing will ever qualify it, nothing will ever interrupt it. And that's what the Lord's people can look forward to in heaven. They can look forward to the fulness of joy in the Lord's presence. As I was trying to say last week, it's a wonderful joy—it can survive the Lord's presence. And it's a wonderful joy that finds its reason—its source—in the Lord's presence. Have we got a joy that can survive his presence? Or is our joy the kind of joy that would evaporate if the Lord were to appear, if we were to be convinced of his presence? Does our joy originate with God? Can we say that there is nothing, and there is no one, that can fill us with satisfaction and gladness in the way that God can do? That was what the psalmist was saying in psalms like Psalm 42 and Psalm 43—he was showing that he had fellowship with God, in the very fact that the absence of God was taking away the joy that he had.

Well, the apostle is speaking about people here in this world and he wants the Lord's people to be rejoicing in God their Saviour. 'Rejoice in the Lord alway: and again I say, Rejoice' (Philippians 4:4). Rejoice in God! Be satisfied with him! Praise him! Think a lot about him, and give honour to him! And take courage from the confidence you have, that he is your God and that you are his people. This is the purpose of Scripture. Scripture makes it possible for us to know Christ in the way that John knew him, and to have fellowship with God and with his Son Jesus Christ, and to have joy, to be full of joy, full of pleasure, at the thought of God. The more Christ is real to us, the more we have communion with him, the more we are relying upon him and the more we are drawing from his fulness, the more we will enjoy God. Man's chief end is to glorify God and to enjoy him for ever, and the Scriptures are the means of making that a reality in the experience of a sinner.

Well then, we should ask ourselves what the Scriptures mean to us. We are all very familiar with them. Perhaps our Bibles open naturally in certain places which we look at particularly frequently. Perhaps our minds are full of them and we could pass an examination in scriptural knowledge. But what we have to ask ourselves is, are we coming to the Scriptures as the infallible Word of God? And when we come to them, are we looking for Christ? Are we searching the Scriptures to find Christ? Are we saying, Oh that I knew where I might find him! that he would be made a reality to me, and that through the experience of that reality I might have fellowship with the Father and with the Son—that I might be truly dependent on God, his love, his redeeming grace, his regenerating power, his sanctifying grace—that I might live the life that I now live in the flesh by the faith of the Son of God? That's the way to joy, that's the way to glorify and enjoy God.

When you look at Psalm 119, for example, you see how the psalmist was living in the atmosphere of the Word of God. He uses so many different words—judgments and precepts and laws and so on. It is as if he was breathing in that atmosphere. That is what accounted for his religion, that is what gave him his knowledge of God and his fellowship with God. And that's what we should be seeking for ourselves, that the purpose of Scripture would be fulfilled in our experience, and that through the gracious working of the Holy Spirit we might have the knowledge of Christ, and the fellowship with God and his Son, and the joy of God, the joy of his salvation in our hearts. 'Search the scriptures; for in them ye think ye have eternal life: and they are they which testify of me' (John 5:39).

May the Lord bless his Word.

5

Themes in 1 John

Fellowship with God

1 JOHN 1:5-7

This then is the message which we have heard of him, and declare unto you, that God is light, and in him is no darkness at all. If we say that we have fellowship with him, and walk in darkness, we lie, and do not the truth: but if we walk in the light, as he is in the light, we have fellowship one with another, and the blood of Jesus Christ his Son cleanseth us from all sin.

LORD'S DAY MORNING, 6TH APRIL 2008

When we were trying to look at the first four verses of this chapter last Sabbath, we tried to consider the light which they throw on the nature of Scripture, namely that while it is written by people who had themselves experience of the truth, what gives it its authority is the fact that they are communicating what has been given to them by God. And then we tried to think a little about the content of Scripture, and particularly how that content is centred on the Lord Jesus Christ. And the third thing we considered was the purpose of Scripture—the particular purpose that the apostle mentions here is that through Scripture, through it being blessed to us by the Holy Spirit, we can come to have that same knowledge of Christ which the apostles had, and we can have fellowship with Christ and with his Father.

I don't intend to try to work all the way through the Epistle, but I feel we ought today to consider these verses.

1. First of all, to notice what they say concerning the nature of God. 'God is light, and in him is no darkness at all.'

2. And then to consider the conditions of fellowship with God. It's a wonderful thing that sinners can have fellowship with God through the Lord Jesus Christ and by the work of the Spirit, but the apostle speaks about conditions of that fellowship: not walking in darkness but walking in the light.

3. The third thing is how that fellowship is maintained. It is maintained by the application of the cleansing blood of Christ to the soul. Those who walk in the light, those who have fellowship with God, are very conscious of the sin that rises up as a barrier between themselves and God. But here is the provision that has been made, the means of maintaining this fellowship: 'the blood of Jesus Christ his Son cleanseth us from all sin.'

1. The nature of God

Now, the nature of God is something that we can only know in a very limited way. It's something that's described in different ways in the Bible. There is no one word which can convey to us the character of God, the nature of God. The particular expression that the apostle is using here is, 'God is light, and in him is no darkness at all.'

We must remember that the apostle's purpose in writing this Epistle was to encourage the assurance of believers—to assure them that they had fellowship with God, to enable them to rejoice in that fellowship. If you and I were going to try to accomplish that aim with someone, we would perhaps be inclined to start with what might seem to be the more encouraging aspects of God's character. We would start by saying, 'God is love.' But before the apostle says 'God is love,' he says, 'God is light, and in him is no darkness at all.' He is not going to lower the conception of God in order to encourage us to think we have fellowship with him if we don't. The God with whom we have fellowship is this God who dwells in light which is inaccessible and full of glory, the God who *is* light. John is emphasising the character of God so that no one is going to be deluded into thinking that God makes any concessions, that God lowers himself in any way, that God compromises in any way, in order to admit sinners into fellowship with him.

This idea of light is one which is frequently connected with God in the Bible. The very first recorded words that God spoke are, 'Let there be light' (Genesis 1:3). And the very last description we have in the Bible of heaven is, 'there is no night there'—they don't need a candle, they don't need the light of the sun, for the Lord God giveth them light (Revelation 22:5). Whatever kind of light it is—natural light, spiritual light, the light of eternal glory—it all originates with God. God *is* light, and every other kind of light is derived from him.

What does the apostle mean when he says, 'God is light'? I suppose various things come to mind in connection with the way that 'light' is used in the Bible. It emphasises perhaps the invisible nature of God. You see things in the light, but the light itself is not something that you see, in that sense. God is invisible, God is transcendent. He is above those things with which we are familiar. God is incomprehensible, God is unapproachable. That's one use that's made of light. He dwells in light inaccessible and full of glory.

But perhaps what is particularly emphasised is the spotless purity and holiness of God, his positive holiness. God is 'glorious in holiness' (Exodus 15:11). When we think of holiness, we really can only think of it as the absence of that with which we are familiar: the absence of sin, the absence of impurity, the absence of inconsistency. And the apostle brings that out. 'God is light, and in him is no darkness at all.' We know what darkness is spiritually. We know what sin is, we know what impurity is, we know what inconsistency is, and imperfection. Take all the evil things we know, and when we think of God, we are thinking of a glorious person who is absolutely free from all these things.

But the holiness of God is not just the absence of unholiness. It's not just the absence of sin and all these other evidences of sin. It is a positive purity, a positive holiness—so much beyond what creatures can have, that holy creatures veil their faces in his presence. That is something that brings home to us that the holiness of God is not just the holiness of a creature multiplied to infinity, but the holiness of

God is something utterly beyond what the holiness of a creature could ever be, magnified however much you might possibly imagine. And that is why creatures who have never sinned, creatures who have always been in the presence of God—who love him with all their hearts, who obey him perfectly, who don't know what sin is experimentally—they veil their faces in his presence. His holiness is majestic and glorious. It's infinite, it's eternal, it's unchangeable. It's just the manifestation of what he is himself. It's not something added to him. It says in Psalm 104 that he has clothed himself 'with light as with a garment' (verse 2). He dwells in light which is inaccessible, unapproachable and full of glory. But that light in which he dwells, that light with which he clothes himself, is not something that's derived from outside of him, it's just the manifestation of what he is. 'God is light, and in him is no darkness at all.'

But you see, that light is manifest. It has been revealed, it has come to expression, in the person of Christ. He said, 'I am the light of the world' (John 8:12). He came to enlighten the darkness of the heathen world. He came to make God known. And when you think that God is light as he is manifest in Christ, you see this other aspect of light—light bringing knowledge, bringing grace, bringing salvation, bringing joy into the experience of sinners. The light of God manifested in Christ shows up our sinfulness, it shows up our corruption, our darkness. But it also makes God known in a way that we can comprehend. We can comprehend the incomprehensible God to the extent to which he has revealed himself in Jesus Christ, and he has revealed himself there as the source of blessing.

You see, when you think of light, you think of knowledge and you think of blessedness, you think of purity. And all these things are brought from God to sinners by the Lord Jesus Christ. So although this description of God, 'God is light,' is one which initially brings home to us our own darkness and sinfulness, yet when you continue to consider it, you discover that the very fact that God has revealed himself in this way is a source of hope and encouragement. The God who commanded the light to shine out of darkness hath shined in our hearts, to give the light of the knowledge of the glory of God *in the face of Jesus Christ* (2 Corinthians 4:6). That's what makes the light a source of blessing: it's shining to us through the Lord Jesus Christ. It's still the light of holiness, but it's the light of grace and hopefulness and blessedness and joy. It's a joyful thing to see the light.

Well, when we think of God—and we *should* think of God—we have to think of him as the one who is glorious in holiness and the one who is glorious in grace. That's where all our thoughts have to begin. That's where John begins. 'This is the message that we have heard of him.' This is what Christ commissioned us to preach. This is what we saw in him himself, in his character, in his words, in his actions, in his life, in his death. God is light. It begins with God. And we have to begin with God. If we're going to get a right sense of sin, if we're going to understand what it means to be a sinner, if we're going to know salvation, if we're going to enjoy the blessedness of salvation, we must begin with God, otherwise our views of sin and salvation will be false. God is the starting place in all our thinking.

God is the starting place in the gospel. It all originates with him, it all centres on him, it's all for his glory. The nature of God is not something that has to be left to theologians to consider in their studies—it is something we have to come face to face with ourselves. In our relation to God in our lives and in our prospects for eternity, we have to face the fact of God. We have to face up to the truth concerning God—we have to believe that God is, that God is light. Yes, he *is* love, he *is* a Spirit, he *is* a consuming fire. What he *is* is described in many ways. But this is something that the apostle is bringing to bear on us, as he endeavours to encourage sinners. We might be thinking, 'If we could just get away from thinking about God, we could perhaps have more comfort.' But the apostle is teaching us that the comfort that comes through getting away from the thought of God is not true comfort at all. You have to face the fact of God, and you have to take things from there. You have to consider yourself in relation to that fact, you have to estimate your own condition in relation to that fact. 'God is light, and in him is no darkness at all.'

2. The conditions of fellowship with God

Well, the second thing that comes before us here is the conditions of fellowship with God. 'If we say that we have fellowship with him, and walk in darkness, we lie, and do not the truth. But if we walk in the light, as he is in the light, we have fellowship one with another.'

What a wonderful thing to think of—a sinner on earth having communion with God! God communicating grace and the soul responding in love, in obedience and in faith towards God—a cóming and going between God and the sinner, seeing things in the same way, enjoying God's favour and seeking to glorify him. 'This is life eternal, that they might know thee, the only true God, and Jesus Christ whom thou hast sent' (John 17:3). That's what he was speaking about in a previous verse: 'Our fellowship is with the Father, and with his Son Jesus Christ.' Christianity—the gospel of the Bible, the religion of the Bible—is not just something cerebral, it's not just something in your head and something in your way of life. When you look at other religions, one thing that is lacking—many things are lacking, many things are false—but one thing that is lacking is this personal fellowship with God. What personal fellowship with their god does the Muslim have? What personal fellowship with God does the modern Jew have? It's all in the head and in the life—it's all believing certain things and doing certain things.

Of course, the religion of the Bible is very much based on believing the doctrines that have been revealed, and the religion of the Bible very much demands living life in accordance with the doctrines and the precepts of the Word of God. But there is something between that belief in the doctrine and that practice in the life, and that is the personal experience of the grace of God and personal fellowship with God through Jesus Christ. Where is the Muslim? Where is the Jew? Where is any religionist, who does not believe in the Lord Jesus Christ, who can enter in experimentally to what Jesus was setting before his disciples when he taught them to pray, 'Our Father, which art in heaven'? There's fellowship at the heart of the gospel—fellowship with God, fellowship with his Son

Jesus Christ, fellowship through his Holy Spirit. And that fellowship is grounded in grace. The initiative is with God. The foundation has been made by God. It's brought about by God's gracious Spirit.

But where that fellowship is, there are certain conditions that prevail—they do not walk in darkness, and they walk in the light.

The first condition of that fellowship is that they do not walk in darkness. If a person says he has fellowship with God and he walks in darkness, he's telling lies and he's not doing the truth. His claim is false. He can't have fellowship with God who is light, and walk in darkness.

Now of course 'walking in darkness' is an expression that has to be taken in its context. It doesn't mean that the person who has fellowship with God will never 'walk in darkness' providentially or spiritually. Remember what it says in Isaiah chapter 50, 'Who is among you that feareth the Lord, that obeyeth the voice of his servant, that walketh in darkness, and hath no light?' Perhaps you're going through a very dark spiritual patch, you're going through a very dark providential experience—you may be like Job and you feel it's all darkness—you can't see God, you can't understand what is happening to you, you don't see any light at the end of your tunnel. The Lord's people go through experiences like that. But that's not what the apostle is saying when he speaks about walking in darkness.

Neither is he saying that the child of God will not be conscious of darkness within himself—spiritual darkness. In fact, if we walk in the light as he is in the light, we will be seeing such darkness in ourselves, such ignorance and error and sin, that it will make us ashamed of ourselves. How can I appear before God? How can I think of speaking about having fellowship with God, when I feel so ignorant of him, I feel so inconsistent with him, I see so much sin in my heart and in my life? That's not what the apostle is talking about either, because the Lord's people, as the apostle goes on to say himself, have to face the fact of their own sinfulness. If we say that we have no sin we are deceiving ourselves. And if we know that we have sin it's going to make us very gloomy when we think about it. 'I see another law in my members, O wretched man that I am!' (Romans 7:23-24). That's not what the apostle is talking about either.

And he's not even talking about a lapse in the life of the child of God. The child of God sins, falls into sin, and is made penitent on account of sin and desires to be delivered from it.

But this is talking about *walking* in darkness—a habitual course of sin, living in the habit of sin, living in the love of sin, living in the practice of sin, and really trying to get away from God, trying to hide the truth about oneself from oneself and from God. That's the kind of thing that is involved in walking in darkness—thinking and living in a way that is inconsistent with God and inconsistent with fellowship with God. The love of sin, and the practice of sin, and the hiding of the truth from God—these are things which are not consistent with walking in the light, not consistent with having fellowship with God. 'If we say that we have fellowship with him, and walk in darkness, we lie, and do not the truth.' If we are living as the unregenerate live, if we are living as if God was not a reality to us, if we are living out of harmony with his revelation and his will for his people, and if this is the course in which we are set, then our claim to have fellowship with God is false. Can two walk together, except they be agreed? What fellowship has righteousness with unrighteousness? What communion has light with darkness?. That's the force of what the apostle is saying here. You cannot be walking in fellowship with God who is light, and be at home in the darkness of sin, living as if there was no God and as if God was not present and God was not observing.

So that is the negative side of this condition of having fellowship with God. This fellowship cannot be had by those who walk on in darkness, those whose carnal mind is enmity against God, those who love sin, those who set the Lord's commandments aside. That's what the Lord says in Psalm 50—you're taking my covenant in your mouth and yet you're ignoring my commandments! How inconsistent! Of course we're full of inconsistencies, but this is an inconsistency that marks a person out as false—not that they sin, but that they live in sin, and they love sin and they don't repent of sin. And if they say they have fellowship with God in that situation, they are telling lies, and they are not doing the truth. They're not *doing* the truth. You remember the solemn words that the Lord spoke in Matthew chapter

7. Many will *say* to me in that day, Lord, Lord, have we not prophesied in thy name? and in thy name have cast out devils? and in thy name done many wonderful works? And then will I profess unto them, I never knew you: depart from me, ye that work iniquity. They will *say*, but what did they *do*? We've got a common saying, 'actions speak louder than words,' and the sentiment is perfectly biblical.

The second condition of fellowship is that they walk in the light as he is in the light. If we are truly in fellowship with God, we will be walking in the light. 'If we walk in the light as he is in the light, we have fellowship one with another.' Walking in the light. God is a reality to us. In the light of that reality we see our own sinfulness and we bemoan our own sinfulness. In the light of that reality we endeavour to live soberly and righteously and godly in this present world. We desire his favour. We desire his presence and blessing. We desire to be frank and open in our dealings with God.

You remember what we have in John chapter 3 about light and darkness. 'He that believeth on him is not condemned: but he that believeth not is condemned already, because he hath not believed in the name of the only begotten Son of God. And this is the condemnation, that light is come into the world, and men loved darkness rather than light, because their deeds were evil. For every one that doeth evil hateth the light, neither cometh to the light, lest his deeds should be reproved. But he that doeth truth cometh to the light, that his deeds may be made manifest, that they are wrought in God.' Those who are walking in the light are often afraid of what they will discover and they are afraid of what God is seeing in them. But instead of scurrying away into some dark corner to get away from the truth concerning themselves, they come to the light. They ask the Lord to search them and try them, to make known the truth concerning them, to see if there is any wicked way in them and to lead them in the way everlasting (Psalm 139:23-24). You see, that's an aspect of walking in the light as he is in the light—coming to God and finding the truth concerning ourselves in the light of what God is, and what God has revealed in his Word.

Of course, there is much more to it than that. Walking in the light is living in accordance with the Lord's revealed will and seeking to be in conscious communion and fellowship with him. It's a life. Just as the life described as walking in darkness is a life characterised by the dominion of sin, so the life of one who is walking in the light is a life characterised by the dominion of grace, the dominion of truth, the dominion of holiness. God is a reality to that person, and the sin, the darkness, the inconsistencies, are a burden to that person. That's the difference—the great difference—between walking in darkness and walking in the light. And we're being told here that the condition of fellowship is walking in the light. Can two walk together, except they be agreed?

3. The means of maintaining this fellowship

Well then, we have to ask, thirdly, how this fellowship is maintained—the means of maintaining this fellowship. When a person walks in the light as God is in the light, that person becomes very conscious of sin. The sense of sin is something that remains with the child of God as long as they are in this world. And perhaps it is something that deepens. Some people begin their spiritual experience of grace with great convictions. Others have much greater convictions some time down the way, after the Lord has brought them to himself. But whatever way the Lord works in his grace, we believe that the Lord's people will have a sense of sin as long as they are in this world—a sense of sin that may not always be as terrific as once it might have been, but which will be deeper and purer in the sense that they will be seeing it as against God, and they will be seeing it is a horrible thing, a loathsome thing. It is not just something that is destructive; it is something that is evil, it is an evil and a bitter thing. Perhaps—not always, but perhaps—we begin our experience of the sense of sin with an emphasis on the bitterness of it, the awful consequences that it brings. But perhaps as the Lord continues to deal with us, we become more impressed with the evil of it, and we see the evil of it in that it is against God, a God of such purity and such goodness.

And when we see something of our own sinfulness, and we have this desire to be in fellowship with God, we become conscious of how sin erects a barrier between us and God—a barrier which must exist, because God cannot tolerate sin. Evil cannot dwell with him, fools cannot stand in his sight (Psalm 5:4-5). And no wonder Isaiah felt the way he did. It was a manifestation of holy grace that he saw in the temple, but he felt so excluded by his sin. 'Woe is me! for I am undone (I am finished); because I am a man of unclean lips, and I dwell in the midst of a people of unclean lips: for mine eyes have seen the King, the Lord of hosts.' (Isaiah 6:5). 'I can't praise him, I want to praise him, I want to join these creatures who are saying, "Holy, holy, holy," but I can't because of my sin. My sin is excluding me. I'm unclean.' Of course, that is the meaning of 'unclean' in the Old Testament dispensation—disqualified from God's presence, God's worship and even the presence of God's people, on account of sin.

And the people who feel that disqualification are those who are walking in the light. How can they have fellowship with God? How can fellowship with God be maintained by people who, the more they get to know God, the more sinful they feel? Well, here is the provision made for sinning believers. 'The blood of Jesus Christ his Son cleanseth us from all sin.' This is not a licence to sin. 'I write these things unto you that ye sin not' (1 John 2:1). This is an encouragement to holiness, an encouragement to repentance, an encouragement to sinners who *are* repenting. There is cleansing for the person who is walking in the light. There is cleansing for the person who is honest in dealings with God, who is confessing sin to God, who truly desires to be in fellowship with God. There is cleansing, there is deliverance from the guilt of sin in the sight of God.

You see, the conscience is purged, but what purges the conscience is what first of all makes atonement to God for sin. Sometimes people would like to get a clear conscience and one way or another they manage to get it. But getting a clear conscience, a conscience rid of the sense of sin at any cost, in any way, is very dangerous, because it's not dealing with the root problem, which is our sin in the sight of God. The only way a conscience can be really purged, purified, pacified, without the person being under a delusion, is when that purging is the consequence of God being satisfied by the atonement that was made by Christ.

That's brought out in the Old Testament in Leviticus. If you look at chapters 16 and 17, you find the emphasis there on the priest making atonement so that people might be cleansed from sin. It's the blood that makes atonement for the soul. The blood of bulls and goats and the ashes of an heifer couldn't take away sin (Hebrews 9:13 and 10:4). They had a certain limited function. They were the means whereby a person could be restored to fellowship with the people of God and the worship of God and so on, and they were pointing forward to a better sacrifice. But what really has efficacy is the blood of Christ, who through the eternal Spirit offered himself without spot to God. *That* purges the conscience from dead works to serve the living God, because it satisfies the demands of God's justice. It's the person he is that gives value to what he has done. No other person could have done what he did. He is the Saviour of his people from their sins. He was appointed to that and anointed for that by God. He is God's own Son. He is God and man in two distinct natures and one person for ever. He had the capacity, the qualification and the power to do what had to be done and he did it. It's the blood that makes atonement. We speak about the sacrifice that he offered on the cross—it wasn't his incarnation that saved sinners from their sins, it wasn't his life of perfect obedience that saved sinners from their sins. It is only because he was incarnate he was able to be a Saviour and it was only because of his perfect obedience he was able to be a Saviour. But he was obedient unto *death*, even the death of the cross. And that's where the power to save lies. The Son of Man has power to forgive sins. The power is in the blood. The power is in the atonement that was made by Christ on the cross of Calvary. It washes sin away out of God's sight so that sin will no longer rise up to condemn those for whom Christ died. What a glorious gospel is the gospel of the blood of Jesus Christ God's Son! That's at the centre of it, it is fundamental to it. 'We joy in God through our Lord Jesus Christ, by whom we have now received the atonement' (Romans

5:11)—the reconciliation, based on the satisfaction that was given to justice.

And this blood cleanseth us from all sin. From *all* sin! 'Justified from all things, from which ye could not be justified by the law of Moses' (Acts 13:39). There were sins under the law, and no sacrifice could save a person from death on account of these sins. But it's not like that with the blood of Christ. There is no exception! Anyone who comes under the shelter of the blood is cleansed from all sin. The blood of Jesus Christ *cleanseth* us from all sin—it's got permanent efficacy. It keeps on cleansing us from all sin, from every single sin that is ours—not just the sins we know and confess, but all those sins which we are so ignorant of because of our sinfulness. We think we're bad enough, but if we only saw ourselves as God sees us! But it's as God sees us this is operating—not from all the sin we confess, not from all the sin we know, not from all the sin we fear is in us, but from all the sin we have—the sin of our nature, the sin of our past, our present, our future. The blood of Jesus Christ his Son cleanseth us from all sin. That's what maintains fellowship. That's how a person can walk in the light, how a person can come to God, how a person can open themselves up before God frankly, confess all the sins that he had known of in his life, because he is coming under the shelter of this provision. The blood of Jesus Christ his Son cleanseth us from all sin.

'We have fellowship with him.' Sin breaks the fellowship, but here is provision to go with our sin to this fountain which is open for sin and for uncleanness. And isn't that what happens? Isn't that what happens in the experience of the Lord's people? 'Iniquities, I must confess, / prevail against me do: / but as for our transgressions, / them purge away shalt thou' (Psalm 65:3). It's not easy. It's easy to say it, but it's not an easy thing to believe it. It wasn't an easy thing to do. It required the atonement that was wrought out by Christ. We confess our sins and we confess them penitently, and we confess them under the shelter of the blood of Jesus Christ, God's Son. That's the meeting place. That's the foundation of fellowship between God and his people. That's what makes it possible for two to walk together. What they are most agreed on is the need for and the power of the blood of Jesus Christ, God's Son. That's where God and his people meet, that's what permits them to walk together, that's how this poor sinner complaining of his darkness can walk in the light—because God and that sinner are agreed that the means of maintaining this fellowship is to be found in the atoning work of the Lord Jesus Christ.

In the Christian life we continue and we end where we began. We come to the cross, we come to the fountain which is opened for sin and for uncleanness. We are as dependent today as we ever were on the atoning work of Christ. It's quite remarkable that, at the very centre of the picture that is given us of heaven in the Bible, is the Lamb in the midst of the throne. That's the foundation of the ongoing communion and fellowship of his people with God. It's built on the acceptable sacrifice which the Lord Jesus offered on the cross of Calvary.

Well then, this is the way that the apostle is encouraging the Lord's people. He is confronting them with the truth concerning God. We have to start there. If we don't start right, we'll not finish right. We may try other starting places, but in our dealings with God we have to begin with facing up to the truth concerning God, concerning his absolute holiness and concerning his wonderful grace, his readiness to make himself known as a holy God in bringing salvation to sinners.

And then, if we are enquiring into how it is between ourselves and God, whether we have fellowship with him, are we united to him, is he our God, are we his people?—then we have to enquire as to how we are walking and where we are walking. Are we walking in darkness, or are we walking in the light? The strange thing is that the person who is walking in darkness in this way might feel that everything is fine, and the person who is walking in the light might feel that everything is wrong. If you're walking in the real dark you don't see that any minute you might be going over the edge of a precipice. If you are walking in the light you see all the alarming things that are round about you. But that's why we have to be clear as to what it means to walk in the darkness and walk in the light. Are we living in the love of sin? Or are we living in the light of the reality of

God, what God is, what God demands, what God has provided in the gospel?

Then of course the ultimate question arising from this is, what use we make, what knowledge we have, of the blood of Jesus Christ his Son cleansing us from all sin. What do we do with our sins, when we are convinced of sin? Do we deny them? Do we try to cover them? Do we try to ignore them? Or do we confess them and come to Christ with them? I mentioned often before how Luther was tempted—the temptation, in his own mind, took this form, that the devil came to him with a long list of his sins. And he asked the devil, 'Is that all? Are there any more to add to it?' Then he said to him, 'Write over them all, "The blood of Jesus Christ his Son cleanseth us from all sin."' And I've also often mentioned and often think about James Lang, that boy in Dundee in McCheyne's time, who died when he was 13. He had quite a while on his death bed, and he had a particular time of depression. But he explained to the minister when he visited him how he got out of that depression. He said, 'The devil was telling me that this word and that word in my prayer was sin, but,' he said, 'I just told him that it is all sin, but that I have taken Christ to be my Saviour, and I told him to go to him, because there is no sin in him.' That's the gospel way. It's so simple to express, yet everything in our nature is against believing it and doing it. We need the power of God's grace to bring us to that point where we confess that it's all sin, and we can't change the fact, we can't modify it, we can't deny it. But this is what we have to do. This is the work of God, that ye believe on him whom he hath sent—that you come to the fountain which is open for sin and for uncleanness, that you pray with the psalmist, although he was using the language of the ceremonial law: 'Do thou with hyssop sprinkle me, / I shall be cleansed so.' (Psalm 51:7). Finlay Cook spoke about the hyssop: 'Dip the hyssop of the promise in the blood of Christ.' Come with his promise, plead his promise, plead *this* promise, that 'the blood of Jesus Christ his Son cleanseth us from all sin.' No one who makes that their refuge will ever be disappointed.

May the Lord bless his Word to us.

6

Themes in 1 John

Sin

1 JOHN 1:8-10

If we say that we have no sin, we deceive ourselves, and the truth is not in us. If we confess our sins, he is faithful and just to forgive us our sins, and to cleanse us from all unrighteousness. If we say that we have not sinned, we make him a liar, and his word is not in us.

LORD'S DAY MORNING, 13TH APRIL 2008

When we were trying to look at the first four verses of this chapter, we endeavoured to consider (1) the light which they throw upon the nature of Scripture, as a testimony from God, and then (2) the content of Scripture, which was centred on Christ, and (3) the purpose of Scripture, which was to bring the readers of Scripture through the blessing of God to have that same knowledge of Christ and fellowship with God which the apostles themselves had.

And then, when we were trying to look at verses 5, 6 and 7, we were trying to think about (1) the nature of God, as that is expressed in the statement, 'God is light,' (2) the conditions of fellowship with God, walking in the light as he is in the light, and (3) the means of maintaining that fellowship, seeing that we are sinners—'the blood of Jesus Christ his Son cleanseth us from all sin.'

What we are confronted with in these closing verses of this chapter is:

WITH AN EVERLASTING LOVE

1. First of all, the nature of sin. We have to think about what sin is. 'If we say we have no sin'; 'if we say we have not sinned'; 'if we confess our sins'—sin is the prominent subject in these verses.

2. And then secondly, the wrong way of dealing with sin.

3. And finally, the right way of dealing with sin.

1. The nature of sin

Sin is a very prominent subject in the Bible. It's not something that's very popular, but it is certainly something that's very prominent in the Word of God. The law of God is continually confronting us with sin, and unless sin means something to us, the gospel will mean nothing to us. People who don't recognise themselves as sinners are not going to appreciate Christ, they're not going to appreciate the gospel. So the gospel itself appeals to the sense of sin.

When we ask ourselves, 'What is sin?' the apostle has already given us some indication of its essential nature. God is light, and if we walk in darkness, we cannot have fellowship with him. Sin is the very antithesis of God and of God's holiness. Sin is being contrary to God. It's alienation from God. It's enmity against God. We can't understand what sin is, except in relation to God. If we think of it just in terms of its effects on us, if we think of it just in relation to other people, we have no true sense of sin. The essential point about sin is that it's against God, and against him only (Psalm 51:4).

And it's against the revelation which he has given of his own will, in his law. You see, that's the significance of the law of God. It's not an arbitrary catalogue of requirements—it's an expression of what God's holiness demands of us. When God says, 'Thou shalt have no other gods before me,' when he says, 'Remember the sabbath day, to keep it holy,' when he says, 'Thou shalt not kill,' he is saying, 'Be thou holy, for I am holy.' He's calling upon us to be conformed to his law. And the fundamental nature of his law, the fundamental principle of his law, is, 'Thou shalt love the Lord thy God, with all thy heart, and with all thy soul, and with all thy mind, and with all thy strength. And thou shalt love thy neighbour as thyself' (Mark 12:30-31). The requirement of God for obedience to his law is a requirement to be conformed to himself, to love himself, to be subject to himself, in every aspect of our lives. And sin, as our Shorter Catechism reminds us, is any want of conformity unto, or transgression of, the law of God. 'Sin,' says John, 'is the transgression of the law' (1 John 3:4). Where there's no law, there's no transgression (Romans 4:15). And we will not begin to appreciate the nature of sin until we see it—till we see all our actions, all our thoughts, all our words—till we see our nature—in the light of the holiness of God, and in the light of the demands of God on us for holiness—a holiness which has love for God as its fundamental characteristic and principle.

You notice how the apostle here speaks about 'sin' in the singular in verse 8, and 'sins' in the plural in verse 9. We believe that in verse 8 he's speaking of sin in the nature—sin as the characteristic, the disposition, of the sinner. It's not just that we do things wrong although basically we're quite in order, we're quite right. The fact is that we are sinners by nature. We fell in Adam, and we have inherited a sinful nature. As soon as we begin to be, we are sinners. The sin of our nature comes to expression in our disposition, in our attitude, in our will, in our affections, in our conscience, in our minds—in every aspect of our being. We have to see, behind the wrong that we do, the evil of our nature—we have to see the corruption, the pollution, of our nature, our lack of original righteousness. We don't have a spark of holiness in us by nature, we don't have a spark of love to God. Our carnal mind *is* enmity—and the Bible is very particular: it doesn't say it is *at* enmity, it says it *is* enmity—against God. It's just a bundle of enmity against God, ready to break out into all kinds of transgression.

And when the apostle speaks about 'sins' in verse 9—'if we confess our sins'—he's referring to the way in which the sin of our nature comes to expression in specific actual ways—the thoughts we think, the words we utter, the things we do. These are 'actual transgressions'. 'Actual transgressions' are not just things we do outwardly. Some people may be very circumspect outwardly (and we should be very thankful for the restraining power of God in keeping people from giving vent outwardly to the corruption of their nature).

And yet we can break all the commandments—we do break all the commandments—although we never opened our mouth, although we never moved a hand or a foot. We're breaking the commandments continually, in our thoughts, in our inward attitudes. And if we were to go through all the ten commandments (to speak of nothing more particular), we wouldn't be able to say with regard to any of them, 'I have kept these from my youth up' (Luke 18:21). Not one of them. 'Oh,' you say, 'I never murdered anyone.' Yes, you've murdered many people in your lifetime, by the thoughts that you entertained concerning them. Perhaps just passing thoughts, perhaps just fleeting thoughts—but thoughts that you wouldn't have had if you were holy. And it's the same with all the commandments. We've broken every one of them. Who can understand his errors? (Psalm 19:12). We can't begin to understand our sins.

Well, whether it's the sin of our nature or the actual sins in which that nature manifests itself, we have to acknowledge that sin is against God. That's the essential nature of sin. It breaks fellowship with God, it makes fellowship with God impossible. And that's the great question we have to face. Have we ever seen ourselves to be sinners? We say it often enough. We say it every time we ask a blessing on our food and every time we try to pray. We say it at the beginning, we say it at the end, we say it in the middle as well sometimes. 'We have sinned.' 'We're great sinners.' But are we seeing ourselves as sinners in the light of this, 'Thou shalt love the Lord thy God with all thy heart, and with all thy soul, and with all thy mind, and with all thy strength, and thou shalt love thy neighbour as thyself.'

2. The wrong way to deal with sin

We *have* to deal with sin. We're going to have to deal with sin, one way or another. We can't get away from it.

The sad thing is that when people are confronted with what the Bible has to say about sin, and when conscience bothers them with regard to sin, the natural tendency is to deal with it in a wrong way. That wrong way is hinted at by the apostle when he says, 'If we say we have no sin, we deceive ourselves, and the truth is not in us ... If we say that we have not sinned, we make him a liar, and his word is not in us.' Here are two wrong ways of dealing with sin—saying we have no sin, and saying we have not sinned.

Now, no doubt the apostle had particular people in mind when he wrote these words—particular heretics, perhaps. Some of them were saying, 'We have no sin. We don't have a sinful nature. We've got beyond that. We've reached a state of perfection. We have not sinned.' They were so deluded as to think that they were not guilty of sinning. But others of the heretics of that time were saying, 'Sin is not my responsibility any more.' They had this idea that sin pertained to the body, or the 'earthly' part of a person, but the soul, the spirit, the 'Christian,' as they might call themselves, was not affected, so that the conclusion they reached was the antinomian conclusion that a person is not responsible for his sins. That's the responsibility of the fallen nature, it's the responsibility of the physical nature, or whatever it might be. One way or another, they were denying responsibility—either denying that they *had* sin, or that they'd sinned, or else denying that they were responsible for their sin.

I don't suppose there's anyone here who adheres to these heretical views of sinless perfection or of irresponsibility for sin. I don't suppose there's anyone here who would say what these people were saying, 'I have no sin, I have not sinned.' If we would justify ourselves, our own mouths would condemn us.

But there are people here, and perhaps we can say, all of us here, who are in great danger of saying in other ways, 'I have no sin, I have not sinned.' We can say things without opening our mouths, we can say things by our attitude. And if a person's not concerned about sin, the sin of his nature, or the sins of his life—not ashamed of them, not penitent on account of them, not seeking deliverance from them—that person is saying in effect, 'I have no sin, I have not sinned.' There's nothing to be worried about, there's nothing to be troubled about. Such a person, by a lack of concern and a lack of repentance and a lack of desire for deliverance from the guilt and power of sin is saying it just as *effectively* as the person who actually puts it into words in this heretical form.

And that is something that the Bible brings out very clearly—how our actions speak louder than words, how the attitudes we have towards the truth can say things that we would never put into words. You and I, as long as we had our reason, wouldn't say, 'I have no sin, I have not sinned.' But are we not really saying that when the Bible accuses us of sin, when the Bible tells us what an evil thing sin is, that it's against God, it's so destructive of his honour, destructive of our own souls, it's bringing us down to a lost eternity, to the pains of hell for ever—and we go on as if sin didn't matter. As if that's something we can leave aside. That's saying, 'I have no sin, I have not sinned.'

And if a person's in that condition—they have the law condemning them, and they have the gospel calling on them to repent and to believe on the Lord Jesus Christ, and they go on their way disregarding law and gospel—are not such people greatly deceived? 'If we say we have no sin, we deceive ourselves, and the truth is not in us.'

'We deceive ourselves.' We're misleading ourselves. We're living in a world of make-believe. We're not facing up to reality. We're under a delusion—a self-induced delusion. If sin is not bothering us, if the call to repentance is going over our heads, if the call to come to Christ for salvation is passing us by, without it creating any concern in our souls, we're self-deceivers, we're living in a dream world.

'And the truth is not in us.' We're not honest, we don't have the truth of God in our souls. We're not dealing frankly with ourselves, we're not dealing frankly with God. God desires truth in the inward parts. He desires people to be frank in their dealings with him. God is true, Jesus Christ is the truth, God reveals the truth concerning himself and concerning us and concerning sin. But obviously that truth is not 'in us' if we are saying in effect that we have no sin. The truth has never taken hold of our minds and our hearts. It hasn't made us true in our dealings with God.

What a sad state to be in! Surrounded by the light of the everlasting gospel. The truth of God is round about us. We're confronted with it in the pages of the Bible. And our own conscience is telling us something about it, however defectively. And yet, we're in such a fog of self-deception that we can't see the truth about ourselves—we won't accept it, we won't come to terms with it.

And what's even worse, if we say we have not sinned, 'we make him a liar.' We're contradicting God. Later on in this Epistle, the apostle is speaking about what God has said concerning his Son, and he says, 'He that believeth on the Son of God hath the witness in himself: he that believeth not God hath made him a liar; because he believeth not the record that God gave of his Son' (1 John 5:10). He is saying the same here with regard to sin. If we don't believe what God has to say concerning sin, let us put it in as blunt a form as the apostle does: we are making God a liar. We're following Satan—that's what Satan did in the garden of Eden. He made God a liar. 'Has God said? Even if he has said it, he'll not do it. Don't believe for a moment that God will cast you out of the garden of Eden—he's just trying to keep you from making progress.' And as the Lord Jesus said to the Jews who were refusing to receive him, 'You're just following in the steps of Satan.' He put it very bluntly, again, 'Why do ye not understand my speech? Even because ye cannot hear my word. Ye are of your father the devil, and the lusts of your father ye will do. He was a murderer from the beginning, and abode not in the truth, because there is no truth in him. When he speaketh a lie, he speaketh of his own: for he is a liar, and the father of it. And because I tell you the truth, ye believe me not. Which of you convinceth me of sin? And if I say the truth, why do ye not believe me? He that is of God heareth God's words: ye therefore hear them not, because ye are not of God.' (John 8:43-47).

'I tell you the truth, and you don't believe me,' the Lord is saying. You're just like Satan. You're making God out to be a liar. That's the seriousness of denying our sinfulness. Either God is true or we are true. Let God be true, but every man a liar (Romans 3:4). It's a very serious, solemn accusation for a person to make. People make it without realising the implications of it when they're not concerned about their sin. When God teaches us the truth that is summarised in our catechism, that every sin deserves God's wrath and curse, both in this life and in that which is to come, and we go on as if sin didn't matter, we are saying in effect that God is a liar.

And we are showing that the truth, his Word, is not in us. 'His Word is not in us.' His Word is truth. And his Word makes very clear our sinfulness. And his Word may be in our ears and his Word may be in our memories, but his Word is not in us, in the sense that it hasn't been received by us and it's not operating effectively in our minds and in our hearts, in our consciences, in our wills, in our affections. It's not *in us*. Is the Word of God *in us*? Has it taken hold of our minds and hearts, so that it affects our thinking about God and our thinking about ourselves and about sin and about salvation? 'If we say we have no sin, we deceive ourselves, and the truth is not in us. ... If we say we have not sinned, we make him a liar, and his Word is not in us.' I've mentioned quite a few times before the incident in Geneva, when Haldane was teaching a class regarding the Epistle to the Romans. Merle d'Aubigné, who became the well-known historian, said to him, 'Now I see the doctrine of sin in the Bible.' And Haldane said to him, 'But do you see it in yourself?' And that's the question. We can see it in the Bible. If people read the Bible, they see again and again and again the doctrine that we read in Romans chapter 3, Old Testament and New Testament, Psalms and prophets and histories and Gospels and Epistles and Revelation, and whatever kind of scripture it is, emphasising the sinfulness of man. That's in the Bible. And we can see it there. But are we seeing it in ourselves? Is the Word *in us*?

You see the wrong way of dealing with sin—ignoring it, denying it, not treating it seriously—showing how deceived we are, how destitute we are of the power of the truth within us, how we're opposing ourselves to God, how we're setting up our own thoughts against the thoughts of God and the revelation which God has given in his Word. The gospel is a gospel for sinners—it's a gospel to be preached to every person under heaven who comes within its sound, whether he knows he's a sinner or not. We don't have to ask a person, 'Do you know you're a sinner or not?' before we can preach the gospel to them—because the gospel is often the means of awakening people to a sense of their sin. But the fact of the matter is that no sinner will receive the gospel, no sinner will come to the Saviour, until he sees himself to be a sinner. One of the poets said, 'A sinner is a sacred thing, / the Holy Ghost hath made him so.' It's very unique, a person who sees himself to be a sinner—that fact is accounted for by the work of God the Holy Spirit. As Dr Kennedy said, 'Even God cannot comfort someone who's not mourning.'

3. The right way to deal with sin

Well, the third thing is the right way to deal with sin. And how we should praise the Lord that there is a way to deal with sin, which meets with success! 'If we confess our sins, he is faithful and just to forgive us our sins, and to cleanse us from all unrighteousness.'

There's a door of hope. There's one of these texts that 'Rabbi' Duncan was referring to when he said, 'If you can't find your way into a text where Christ is, get into it through its reference to sin.' We mightn't be able to say *confessing*, we mightn't be able to say *forgiveness*. But *sin* is something that's within our reach, *sin* is something that we know, *sin* is something that opens the door—the fact that this is *for sinners* opens the door of hope for us.

What does it mean to confess our sins? Well, the word that's translated 'confess' we sometimes transliterate from Greek into the English word 'homologate'. It's to 'homologate' what God says—to say the same thing as God says, to assent to what God says, to affirm the truth of what God says, to agree with it, to accept it, and to say it ourselves. That's the essence of confession of sins: to come to have the same view of ourselves, although in a much more limited way, as God has—to think of ourselves as God describes us in his Word. He has said that we have all sinned and come short of the glory of God (Romans 3:23), that there's none righteous, no, not one (Romans 3:10). And he says that to each of us, particularly, in his Word. And when we confess our sins, we're coming to terms with that fact, and we're agreeing with what God has to say about us.

Of course, it's an agreement that is not simply verbal, but it comes from the heart. It's not just *saying*, 'I have sinned.' There are examples, very alarming examples, in the Bible of people who said, 'I have sinned.' King Saul in the Old Testament said, 'I have sinned.'

But his professed confession was shown to be very faulty. He just said it because he didn't want to lose face—he didn't want Samuel to leave him, he didn't want to be dishonoured as a king. He would say anything to keep his reputation, even, 'I have sinned.' And then you have Judas Iscariot, 'I have sinned, in that I have betrayed the innocent blood.'

Yes, we can *say*, 'I have sinned,' but if we really mean it, then it has to come from the heart. And if it comes from the heart, it'll not be a passing phase with us—it will be a continual confession. It's a continuous thing—'if we confess'—if this is our character, if it becomes the habit (if we might use the word) of the renewed life to be confessing sin. And if we're confessing it in that way, it'll be accompanied by repentance and by shame, by self-reproach, self-rebuke. You can't say, 'I have sinned,' in the presence of God, and smile, and laugh, when you're doing so—or think lightly of it, or forget about it the moment you've uttered the words. No, there will be a shame and a sorrow and a repentance in the heart. As Ezra said, 'I'm ashamed, I blush to lift up mine eyes to thee, because we have sinned.' The soul can blush, the soul can be ashamed, on account of sin.

That's the kind of confession of sin that the Bible is requiring of us, and that grace creates in the soul of a sinner. A true sense of sin will make a person ashamed of sin, but not be ashamed to confess that sin. I think again it was probably 'Rabbi' Duncan who said that—that we should be ashamed of our sin, but we should never be ashamed to confess our sin to God.

And look at the great encouragement there is for confession in the absolute assurance that is given. 'If we confess our sins, he is faithful and just to forgive us our sins, and to cleanse us from all unrighteousness.'

There's *forgiveness* with God—the putting away of sin, the sending away of sin. That's literally what it means—to send it away, to dismiss it, to put it out of the reckoning. 'As far as east is distant from / the west, so far hath he / from us removed, in his love, / all our iniquity' (Psalm 103:12). He puts it away so that never again will it be brought up to condemn the sinner.

The thoroughness of this forgiveness comes out in this cleansing *from all unrighteousness*. It's a thorough, comprehensive, lasting deliverance from the guilt of sin, from everything that would make us liable to the sentence of divine justice condemning us to eternal death. It's a thorough, lasting deliverance from sin as guilt which exposes us to the wrath and to the curse of God. And this is the God who has made very clear in his Word that he will by no means clear the guilty (Exodus 34:7). By no means clear the guilty! God doesn't say that the guilty are not guilty. That's not the gospel. We might sometimes misapprehend it as if God is saying, 'Although you are guilty, I'll treat you as if you're not guilty.' That's not it—that's a lie, that's a delusion, it's something made up, something unreal, something God cannot do. He cannot say to the guilty sinner, 'You're not guilty.' But what he does is, he removes the guilt. He takes that guilt away, so that the sinner is not guilty. The guilt has been imputed to Christ. 'The Lord has laid on him the iniquity of us all' (Isaiah 53:6).

And *cleansing* brings that out. When you think of the context in the Old Testament, cleansing was dependent on atonement being made, on blood being shed, on satisfaction being given to the law and justice of God. What we're being assured of here is that the sinner who confesses his sin, who comes to God and acknowledges the truth of his Word and the justice of his condemnation, God is able and God will and God does blot out all that person's sins and transgressions through the atoning sacrifice.

You see, it's against God we've sinned, and the person who's coming to God, confessing his sin, may wonder, 'How can God forgive my sins? Can I really be cleansed from all unrighteousness?' So the apostle, the inspired apostle, is emphasising, 'He is faithful and just to forgive us our sins.'

He is *faithful* to do it. He has said it, and he will do it. He is faithful who has promised. And it's a great guarantee, a great help to a poor sinner, who has no claim upon God's mercy, who has no righteousness to plead before God, for that poor sinner to be assured, 'God is faithful, he's true to himself, he's true to his word, *he* has said it, and he will do it.' And no one will ever be able to stand up in the day of judgment and say, 'I came and I confessed my sin, I cast myself on the mercy of God in Christ Jesus, and I was cast away.' None perish who trust in him. He is faithful, he's true to his word. And he's taken great steps to emphasise that, as we have it in the Epistle to the Hebrews—he could swear by no greater. An oath for confirmation is an end of all strife (Hebrews 6:16). An oath doesn't mean much nowadays in our law courts—people can swear before God and tell downright lies. But that doesn't alter the significance of the oath. The oath is for confirmation, and God wishing to give the heirs of promise a sense of the certainty of his word swore with an oath, and because he could swear by no greater he swore by himself. And that's the confirmation that we have. As sure as God is God, he who confesses his sins will obtain mercy. His sins will be forgiven. He's faithful to do it.

And he's *just* to do it. His righteousness makes it possible—his righteousness demands it. We read that he's *just* and the justifier of him that believeth in Jesus. The justice of God will not stand in the way of a confessing sinner being forgiven—the justice of God *demands* that the confessing sinner must be forgiven. God cannot punish Christ in the place of his people and then punish *them* to all eternity—that would be a gross injustice. What a wonderful gospel we have, that justice as much as mercy is demanding the forgiveness of the sinner who confesses his sins. You don't need to be afraid of the justice of God condemning you if you come to God through Christ, because that justice is just as much for you, and as much for your salvation, as God's mercy is. 'Truth met with mercy, righteousness / and peace kissed mutually' (Psalm 85:10). It's a glorious gospel! God's attributes are always harmonious, but the harmony of them is seen in forgiving the sins of those who believe in Jesus, those who confess their sins over the head of the Lamb of God.

That's the assurance, the encouragement, that is given to poor sinners in this verse. If we confess our sins, he is faithful and just to forgive us our sins, and to cleanse us from all unrighteousness. He is faithful and just. God will cease to be God, he will cease to be true to himself, he will cease to be the righteous one that he is, if any sinner comes to him, confessing his sins, and is not forgiven. We couldn't say these things if God didn't say them himself. And how thankful we should be that God has said them, loud and clear, in the Bible. He's giving us this encouragement, he's giving us this assurance, to encourage us to come and to confess our sins to him.

Of course, that confession will be very limited, in the sense that we don't know much of our own sinfulness. But is it not a great thing that it goes on to say, 'He will cleanse us from *all unrighteousness*'? We confess this sin and that sin, we confess the sinfulness of our nature. But who can understand his errors? Who knows the slightest fragment of his sinfulness, his sinful nature, or his sinful actual transgressions of God's law? We confess our sins, and we do so in a very partial, limited way. But he cleanses us from all our transgressions—the ones we never knew we had, the depths of iniquity that are hidden within us, the thoughts that never occurred to us as being sinful. He cleanses his people from all of them. They're justified from all things—*from all things*—from which they could not be justified by the law of Moses (Acts 13:39).

Now, the last thing to mention is, what is the connection between the confession and the forgiveness? The confession cannot be the cause of the forgiveness. The confession is itself a fruit of mercy. We're not confessing our sins as if confession can secure God's favour, as if it's a work of ours. It's a fruit of the Spirit, it's a fruit of grace, a fruit of the sacrifice of Christ. But there's a link that cannot be broken between confession and forgiveness.

For one thing, there's the objective and the subjective aspects of salvation. We are forgiven, our relationship is put right with God. But when that happens, there's a change that takes place within the soul also, and the soul takes up God's side against sin—the person is renewed inwardly. This is one way of emphasising that fact—it's not that people are forgiven and then they keep on going in the ways of sin as they always did. If we are forgiven then we are also changed by God's grace and sin becomes a hateful thing to us—we want to be rid of it. If we're justified, we'll be sanctified. The faith that we have in the justifying righteousness of Christ comes from God's regenerating work, which makes us hate sin and love holiness.

And of course there is also the fact that they that are whole need not a physician, but those who are sick. Confession is like the person who's come to realise that he is sick and he goes to the physician. It's a way of expressing our absolute dependence on the grace and mercy of the Lord. If we confess our sins, he is faithful and just—he's not going to give his glory to another. Those whom he saves are going to be made to realise that they owe it all to his grace. That's what confession is doing—it's acknowledging, 'I have nothing to bring to thee, I have nothing to commend me, I'm absolutely dependent on thy grace and thy mercy.' It's a way of glorifying God. The soul is saying, 'Yes, I deserve the condemnation that is threatened against me because of my sins.' It's acknowledging our transgression and acknowledging the justice of our condemnation, and giving to God the glory of our salvation. People who are not willing to confess their sins are determined to hold on to their sins and to hold on to their pride. But when a person does confess sins, with shame and with penitence and casting themselves on the mercy of God in Christ Jesus, they're showing that sin has become their burden, and that they really do desire to be rid of it, and to be put right with God, and to have a right relationship, to have fellowship with him. Augustine said on one occasion, 'Do you wish him to forgive you?' then, he said, 'Confess!' That's really what the gospel confronts us with. You're wishing forgiveness? Well, confess! Confess your sins before God, cast yourself on his mercy in Christ Jesus!

If you are confessing your sins, then you have this encouragement, you have this absolute assurance in the Word, that he is faithful and just to forgive you your sins, and to cleanse you from all unrighteousness. You see, getting the Word into our hearts and minds is often the problem. Just as it is with regard to the sense of sin, so it is with regard to the sense of forgiveness. The assurance is there in the Word, but how we need that assurance to be impressed on us by the Spirit of God in our own souls, in our own minds, so that we'll believe that our sins are forgiven!

Well then, what does sin mean to us? Do we have the true biblical view of our own sinfulness? And are we enabled to go with that to Christ, to go with it to God, and to be frank and open and honest in our dealings with him? That's what the psalmist was telling us in Psalm 32—how he was bottling it all up in himself, and apparently over a period—he knew he was a sinner, but he wouldn't confess it, he wouldn't or couldn't repent. But the time came when, 'I will confess unto the Lord / my trespasses, said I.' He was brought to the place where he couldn't cover it up any longer. He couldn't contain it any longer. He had just to open himself up to God and to confess all that he knew about his own sinfulness. And as soon as that happened, God forgave the iniquity of his sin. He didn't put him on probation, didn't send him to purgatory—he forgave his sins, there and then. That's the glory of the gospel. When the sinner comes to confess, he finds God is waiting to be gracious, God is rich in mercy, God is able and willing and does forgive.

May the Lord bless his Word.

7

Themes in 1 John
The advocate with the Father

1 JOHN 2:1-2

My little children, these things write I unto you, that ye sin not. And if any man sin, we have an advocate with the Father, Jesus Christ the righteous: and he is the propitiation for our sins: and not for ours only, but also for the sins of the whole world.

LORD'S DAY MORNING, 20TH APRIL 2008

At the start of the Epistle the apostle wrote about the fact that, through the Scriptures (which are an authoritative testimony to Christ), believers in every generation can come to know Christ, just as the apostles knew him. Also they can have fellowship with the Father and with the Son, and they can have the joy of God's salvation. He also wrote about the glorious being of God—'God is light'—and of the conditions of fellowship with God, and the way in which fellowship is maintained with God, through the blood of Christ cleansing his people from all their sins. And then he wrote about sin itself and about the wrong way to deal with sin and the right way to deal with sin—showing that if people deal with sin in the right way, if they confess their sins, God is faithful and just to forgive them their sins, and to cleanse them from all unrighteousness.

These are the 'things' that he's referring to when he says, 'My little children, these things write I unto you.' And he's making it very clear that his purpose in writing—and of course he was moved by the Holy Spirit—was not to make them feel at ease with regard to their sin. That danger exists. If people somehow get a hold of the ideas of the gospel, they get a hold of the doctrines of grace in their heads and they come to imagine that they are saved by God's grace, they can think lightly of sin, they can feel at ease in sin.

But that is not the case when the doctrines of grace, the doctrines of salvation, are received by faith into the soul of a sinner who has been born again by the Holy Spirit of God. These doctrines of grace which the apostle has been expounding don't encourage people to sin—they dissuade people *from* sin. Think of the Scripture's purpose—to make Christ known and to bring people into fellowship with God. If that purpose is accomplished in the experience of a sinner, that sinner is not going to feel at ease in sin. If a sinner comes to know God as light, and to have fellowship with him, and to be depending on the blood of Christ for that fellowship, that sinner is not going to feel that sin is a light matter. The apostle has been describing sin as that which disrupts fellowship with God, because it's against God—if a person comes to see sin in that way, and comes to confess sin with shame, and to depend on the faithfulness and justice of God for cleansing, then that sinner is not going to think lightly of sin. These doctrines, these truths, when they become realities in a person's experience, fulfil the purpose that the apostle has here—in dissuading people from sin. 'Sin no more,' Christ said (John 5:14). The apostle is speaking with affection. 'My little children.' No doubt he was an old man, and many of these might have been converted through his preaching for all we know, but his affection is just a stream from the affection of God himself, and in his affection he is dissuading them from sin, and using the doctrines to discourage them from sinning.

But the doctrines of the Bible also recognise that Christians *do* sin—that they sin every day. They got a prayer taught to them by the Lord, 'Give us this day our daily bread.' It's a prayer for every day, it's a pattern for our prayers every day, and one of the petitions is, 'Forgive us our debts, as we forgive our debtors.' The apostle is recognising that fact. If we say we have no sin, if we say we haven't sinned, we're deceiving ourselves. We *are* sinners—it's not that we *were* sinners, we *are* sinners—and for those who have been delivered from the guilt of sin and the power of sin, and yet are sinning every day, provision has been made. And the provision is what attention is focused on here. 'If any man sin.' We shouldn't take sin for granted, as if our sin was inevitable and therefore we don't need to be concerned about it, but we do sin. 'And if any man sin, we have an advocate with the Father, Jesus Christ the righteous: and he is the propitiation for our sins: and not for ours only, but also for the sins of the whole world.'

1. As the Lord would enable me, I would like to say a little first of all about those who have an advocate with the Father. Who are those people who can say, 'We have an advocate with the Father?'

2. And secondly, the advocate whom we have with the Father. That of course is the major part of the text. It's not focusing attention on us: it is focusing attention on him.

3. And then in the third place, what effect these truths should have on us—whether we do or do not have the advocate.

1. Who has the advocate?

When we look at this question, 'Who has an advocate with the Father?' we're not looking at the question of who *needs* an advocate with the Father. There's no doubt that we all need an advocate. We all need someone to represent us and speak for us in the court of heaven—to speak for us to God. We have all sinned, and become exposed to the just condemnation of God's holy law. We have all come under the sentence of condemnation. We are all exposed to the wrath and curse of God. And as the apostle Paul said to the Romans, 'By the deeds of the law there shall no flesh be justified in his sight' (Romans 3:20). The law exposes our sin, the law condemns us for our sin, and the law closes our mouths in God's presence. No one is going to get up on the day of judgment and make a big speech about themselves and their goodness. Many people do it today—they can tell the Lord how good they think they are—'I thank thee that I am not as other men are. I may not be what I should be, but I'm better than other people are, and I'm not as bad as I might be, and there's all these circumstances that need to be taken into account, these temptations I have,' and all the rest of it. People find extenuating circumstances, and they present as good a case as they can for themselves. But when they appear before God, the Bible says they'll not be able to open their mouth. All these loud-mouthed sinners will be silent in the day of judgement—not able to speak a word in their own defence. We all need someone to speak for us, or else there'll be no speaking for us in the day of judgment.

And when we ask about who has the advocate, we're not looking at the question of *who is invited to make use* of the advocate. The gospel invites sinners everywhere who hear it to make use of the advocate— and to make use of him without money and without price. Christ is readily available to sinners who wish to make use of him in their approaches to God. There wouldn't be a gospel to preach, if that was not the case. 'This man receiveth sinners' (Luke 15:2). This man has never turned away anyone who came in a state of concern about sin to seek his help, to seek his aid, to seek his intercession with God on his behalf. The Lord Jesus himself is full and free with his invitations. 'Come unto me, all ye that labour and are heavy laden, and I will give you rest' (Matthew 11:28). Come to *me* with your burden of sin, and I will deal with it—I'll take it away, I'll represent you in the court of heaven.

But what we are looking at is, who *has* the advocate? Who needs him, who has heard the invitation to make use of him, and who, now, *has* him representing him in heaven? We have an advocate.

Here are just a few things about these people. And the first thing is, of course, that they have confessed themselves to be sinners. Not just to have *been* sinners, but to *be* sinners, against God. That's what the apostle has been bringing out in the previous verses—that people who have fellowship with God are people who have sins to confess, and who are ready to confess them. And, having been made ready to confess their sins, they have become ready to acknowledge that their sins deserve God's wrath and curse, both in this life, and in that which is to come. They confess that the law has a good case against them. They confess that they are justly exposed to whatever sentence God in his justice may pronounce on them. Their own conscience confirms the sentence of God against them. And when they hear Satan, the accuser of the brethren, saying things about them, they have to acknowledge that what he says is true. They are not able to defend themselves from the accusations of the law, from the accusations of conscience, from the accusations of Satan.

The second thing is that they have heard of the advocate—they've heard of Christ. He's been set before them in the everlasting gospel, and they have been persuaded and they have been enabled to take their case to Christ—to commit their case to Christ. 'I know whom I have believed, and am persuaded that he is able to keep that which I have committed unto him, against that day' (2 Timothy 1:12). They can't speak for themselves. They can't say anything in their own defence. But they are looking to Christ. If Christ will not speak for them, their case is lost for ever. That's how they feel in their own souls. And perhaps you're here today, and you can't go much further than that. But is it not good to have come as far as that? To feel that without Christ you're lost. To feel that if he will not speak for you, you cannot speak for yourself. To feel that your sins deserve God's wrath and curse, and nothing and no one can properly save you from that but the Lord Jesus Christ. Be thankful if you've come to that point!

Thirdly, these are people who are relying on Christ alone for salvation, and it has changed their attitude to sin completely. That's why the apostle is saying, 'That ye sin not'. That's their desire—to hate sin. They can't help confessing it, but they confess it with shame, because they've come to see it in a little measure as God sees it—they've come to hate it. They don't want just to be saved from going to hell, they want to be saved from *sin*, and from *sinning*. That's a great evidence of really believing in the Lord Jesus Christ. 'Thou shalt call his name Jesus, for he shall save his people from their sins' (Matthew 1:21) And that's what you want to be saved from. Yes, you want to be saved from going to hell and you want to be saved from the wrath to come, but not so that, when you'd got the assurance of that salvation, you could sin to your heart's content. No! You want to be delivered. You're praying not only, 'Cleanse me from the guilt of sin,' but, 'cleanse me from the very existence of sin in my soul.' One of the things that makes you look forward to heaven, even when you're afraid you'll never be in heaven, is that it's the place where sin shall be no more—where you'll be free, if you get there, from that accursed thing which is troubling you day and night. Although your external life may be circumspect, you're so conscious of the evil within, and your desire is not just 'Save me from going down to the pit,' but 'Save me from that pit of corruption which is in my own heart.'

These are the people who have an advocate with the Father. They've come to be on the same side of the argument as the Father is himself—to be against sin, to be for Christ, and to be relying on him alone for salvation.

Well, are we among them? Do we have an advocate with the Father? These are not the qualifications for coming to Christ. These are the characteristics of those who have come, and who are coming, every day, to Christ.

2. The advocate with the Father

Well, let us try to consider a little about the advocate whom we have with the Father. 'We have an advocate with the Father, Jesus Christ the righteous, and he is the propitiation for our sins, and not for ours only, but also for the sins of the whole world.'

Well, of course, the Father is the first person of the Godhead. And in the scheme of redemption, in the revelation that has been given of the way of salvation, the Father is, as it were, the guardian of the interests of God. He represents the claims and interests of God. He is also the source of grace and of salvation, who sends his Son, and who sends forth his Holy Spirit.

And 'the Lord our God is holy still' (Psalm 99:9). He is the Father. When one thinks of him as the first person of the Godhead, and one thinks of him as the conservator (as it were) of the rights of the Godhead, and when one thinks of him as the source of grace and salvation and blessing, one must not forget that he is holy. That he is a Father to Christ and a Father to his people does not mean that he has ceased to be the God he was, to be the God he is—infinitely glorious in his holiness. That's why we need an advocate *with the Father*. The Father is not one of these fathers who sees nothing wrong in his children and isn't concerned about their sins and doesn't endeavour to correct them. The Father is holy still.

The advocate is one who is called to us, or called alongside us, in order to help us. The word 'paraclete', as you know, is sometimes translated 'comforter' and in John it's translated as 'advocate.' It has the same meaning as 'advocate' has—'called to.' Here is one who is called to our side in order to help us, in order to defend us, in order to speak for us to God and with God. He is our representative. We have an advocate with the Father. We have this person, who has been appointed to defend us, and he has access to the Father. He is able to practise, he is able to function, in the court of heaven. He has been appointed by the Father. He is qualified and he is prepared to speak for his people, to defend their case before God the Father.

This advocate is set before us in the glorious person that he is— he has been spoken of as 'Jesus Christ his Son,' and now he is spoken of as 'Jesus Christ the righteous'. We know that the name *Jesus* identifies him as a historical person, a person with real humanity. He was born and he grew up, he lived and he died—a person whose appearance in history was in order to save his people from their sins. The fact that he's called *Christ* identifies him as the promised Messiah, as the one who was appointed by God and equipped by God for the work of saving his people. He hasn't just risen up himself, he hasn't taken this honour to himself—he was appointed by God. The fact that he is *his Son* is fundamental also, because no one could do what Jesus Christ has to do if he were a mere man. But he's not a mere man: he is the Son of God, the Word of life manifest, God manifest. 'In the beginning was the Word, and the Word was with God, and the Word was God' (John 1:1). It's his divinity, it's his Godhood, that gives him the capacity to undertake this tremendous work. Godhood and manhood combined in the one person qualify him to be the Saviour. If you think about it, there are things that had to be done by the advocate, by the Saviour, that could not be done by a person who was only God. And there were things which could not be done by a person who was only man. But we have God and man, still with these two distinct natures, but one person, so that what is done by one nature is done by the person, and Jesus Christ the Son of God had the capacity to do everything that was necessary. Everything that required divinity, and everything that required humanity, Christ was capable of doing.

But in this particular text here, he is described as *Jesus Christ the righteous*, the just. No doubt that speaks about the righteousness of his person in the first instance. He is the righteous God, he is a righteous man. He is 'holy, holy, holy, Lord God Almighty' (Revelation 4:8). He is holy, harmless, undefiled, and separate from sinners (Hebrews 7:26). His own personal righteousness was essential to his being able to represent those who were sinners. But particularly, I believe, it's referring to him as the advocate with the Father, Jesus Christ the righteous. He is a righteous advocate.

The righteousness of the advocate, the righteousness of his advocacy, is seen in various ways. For example, it's seen in the fact that he insists on those whom he represents confessing all the sin they know—making a clean breast of their sins. And when he speaks for them to God, he is able to acknowledge sin in them of which they never were aware themselves. And he does so. He doesn't pretend that they are innocent. He's representing them as sinners, and he represents them as sinners to God. And brings out the worst that can be brought out about them. And if we think of it in our own human terms, he tells God everything about them—how wicked they are, in their nature, in their thoughts, in their words, in their actions—he brings it all out into the open, things we could never bring out ourselves. We're worried about the things we see in ourselves—and there's a lot more in us than we ever have seen or ever will see—but the Lord Jesus sees it all, and all of that is brought out by him as the advocate. You never heard of an advocate, or anyone else in a court, telling the court what a wicked person his client was. But that's what the Lord Jesus does. He brings out the worst about them.

And another thing about him which marks out how righteous he is—he insists on the law and justice of God being upheld in its integrity, in its fulness. He will not have any concessions made to the sinner. He magnifies the law and makes it honourable (Isaiah 42:21).

He brings home to their consciences the law of God, and in God's presence he doesn't do anything or say anything that will in any way undermine the claims which the law of God has on them. He's not looking for loopholes in the law, so that they get off on a legal technicality, as we hear about in earthly courts. There are no legal technicalities regarding the law of God that can be used as a loophole to let a criminal escape. The Lord Jesus Christ, in his whole life—in his submission to death on the cross of Calvary, and in his intercession at God's right hand—is asserting the rights of God's law and the rights of God's justice.

And he is on the side of the Father against whom they have sinned. He's in perfect sympathy with the mind of God the judge. Looked at from another angle, he is the judge himself. There's a perfect harmony between the judge on the judgment seat, and the advocate standing before him, representing these sinners.

And yet, the advocate is presenting a case for their acquittal. He is acknowledging how sinful they are, acknowledging the law in its integrity, acknowledging the justice of their condemnation, acknowledging that the Father's view of the matter is perfectly correct. Yet Christ, the advocate, the righteous advocate, is pleading that the case against them will be dismissed, and that they will be acknowledged and acquitted in the day of judgment—acknowledged as righteous in the day of judgment.

One might ask, 'What is the plea, what is the argument, what is the case that he presents?' And it is this: 'He is the propitiation for our sins.' It's not that he comes *with* a propitiation, but that he *is* the propitiation. He is the one who diverts the wrath of God from his people, because he has endured that wrath himself. That's the gospel of the grace of God. It's so out of fashion nowadays! But it's the truth that lies at the heart of the revelation that God has given in the gospel, that the Lord laid on him the iniquities of all his people. He was made sin for them, so that they might be made the righteousness of God in him, he was made a curse for them, so that they might be delivered from the curse of the law. He was always the Son of God's love. And yet, as our representative, as the representative of his people, he became the object of God's wrath. You see, our feeble minds can't comprehend these things—how the one person could be the object of God's eternal love and yet the object of his wrath, and subjected to his curse. We can't comprehend how God could say of him—and could say of him even when he was on the cross, 'This is my beloved Son, in whom I am well pleased,' and yet could say, 'Awake, O sword, against my shepherd, and against the man that is my fellow' (Zechariah 13:7). Viewing Christ in himself, he was the object of God's love. Viewing him as the representative of his people, he was the object of God's love. And yet, as he bore their sins, he experienced the curse of God against them for these sins, and he experienced the wrath of God against them for their sins. And he experienced it in a way that's beyond anything that anyone—or everyone together—will ever be able to comprehend. The saints in heaven will never know what Christ endured, and to all eternity the lost in hell will never know what Christ endured. The person that he was enabled him to endure that wrath to the uttermost, in these comparatively short moments on the cross of Calvary. Yes, 'he was wounded for our transgressions, he was bruised for our iniquities: the chastisement of our peace was upon him; and with his stripes we are healed' (Isaiah 53:5). That is the plea he has to present: the Lamb slain in the midst of the throne, the advocate pleading for their acquittal, because he is the propitiation for their sins.

What a powerful argument that is, considering that God sent him to be the propitiation for the sins of his people! We mustn't think for a moment that Christ was persuading an angry God to be gracious, persuading a God who wanted to curse them to bless them. Sometimes the gospel is misrepresented in that way—those who are the enemies of the gospel may say that here is God intent on destroying people and Christ comes and stands between them and persuades him not to do so. That's not the case. We read later on in this Epistle, in chapter 4, verses 9 and 10, 'In this was manifested the love of God toward us, because that God sent his only begotten Son into the world, that we might live through him. Herein is love, not that we loved God, but that he loved us, and sent his Son to be the propitiation for our sins.' He sent his Son to be the propitiation for our sins—the love of God is manifested in sending Christ to be the mercy seat, to be the one who would come between us and a condemning law, and who would satisfy all the demands of that law and justice of God, and bear the wrath that we deserved, so that we might be delivered from the wrath to come. We have an advocate, a person fully qualified, in himself and in the arguments he has to present, to be the representative of his people, and to secure their deliverance.

And the apostle says something more about him when he declares, 'not for ours only but also for the whole world.' 'He is the propitiation for our sins, and not for ours only, but also for the whole world.' Now that does not mean that Christ either intended to or did secure the salvation of the whole world. It doesn't mean that he endured the wrath that was due to every sinner of mankind. What the apostle is doing is emphasising the uniqueness and the efficacy of Christ's advocacy and Christ's propitiation. What comfort, what encouragement would it be to you or to me today, if we were told that Christ died for everyone, when yet we know that there are multitudes lost for ever? Christ didn't die for everyone.

What the apostle is bringing before us first of all is the fact that this advocate is quite unique. It's not that we have this advocate and other people may have another advocate, some other way of getting to heaven, some other way of getting into the good favour of God. Although that's a common delusion today, it's completely contrary to Scripture. 'There is none other name under heaven given amongst men, whereby we must be saved' (Acts 4:12). There is no salvation in any other. 'I am the way, the truth, and the life: no man cometh unto the Father, but by me' (John 14:6). It may not be popular in our day, but it's the truth of God, and people who believe otherwise are certainly going contrary to the Word of God. There's not a Christian way of getting to heaven and a Muslim way of getting to heaven and a Jewish way of getting to heaven—there's only one way of getting to heaven. That is brought out when he says, 'not for ours only, but for the whole world.' In all the world, there's only one advocate, there's only one propitiation.

But it's also emphasising the efficacy of Christ's advocacy and propitiation. This is a gospel which can be preached everywhere and to everyone. And everyone who comes to Christ and makes use of Christ will find that he'll be an advocate to them, and the propitiation for their sins. It's in Christ the love of God is tasted, it's in Christ the mercy of God is tasted. Christ is the one who saves us from our sins, who saves us from the wrath to come. This gospel can be preached in all the world, to all the nations, to every kind of sinner—to lost and ruined sinners, the chief of sinners, blasphemers and persecutors and injurious. Those who were notorious for their sins can be told that there's a Saviour that is suitable for them, that there's one who is able to save them to the uttermost who come unto God through him, seeing he ever liveth to make intercession for them. It doesn't matter where they came from and it doesn't matter what they were before they came. Those who come to God through him, those who have him as their advocate, as their high priest, as their intercessor—he's able to save them. It's consistent with God's eternal purpose, it's consistent with God's justice, it's something that Christ can do. He can save the chief of sinners.

So, what these words are doing is not diluting the gospel, and making it a possibility rather than a certainty for sinners. Saying that Christ is the propitiation not for our sins only, but also for the whole world, is emphasising just how unique and just how effective an advocate he is, and how effective a propitiation, propitiating God, turning away God's wrath from those who are trusting in him, those who are represented by him.

Well, he's a wonderful person, and he's a wonderful advocate. The apostles cannot speak too highly of him. We wish we would speak much more highly of him than we do. But we can commend Christ to sinners, as a suitable and a sufficient Saviour for them.

3. The effect which these truths should have on us

What effect should these truths have on us?

If we are one of those who commit our case to Christ and trust in him alone for salvation, we have reason in that fact to be cautious with regard to sin. That's the main point that the apostle is making with regard to what he has written previously, but it's also true of what he's writing here: 'These things write I unto you, that ye sin not.' The purpose of writing these things is that we should not sin, that we should hate sin, that we should seek after holiness. If we have an advocate with the Father, if we have been brought to put our sinful case in Christ's hands, then surely it's going to make sin abhorrent to us, and it's going to make us want to live a life free from sin. That's the aim and that's the desire of believers.

It will also mean that there should be a readiness to confess our sins to the Lord. If we have an advocate—if Christ is our advocate—that should encourage us to be full and frank in our confession of sin. If we don't have an advocate, then we want to keep our sins to ourselves as much as we can, and to confess as little as we possibly can. But when we do have an advocate—when we have one who will plead our case—let us confess with shame. As someone said, 'We should confess with shame, but we shouldn't be ashamed to confess our sins to the Lord.'

And if we have an advocate, let us also take comfort from that fact. We are cautious with regard to sin, yet we have sin to confess. Then let us take comfort from the fact that we have an advocate with the Father. Although we can never atone for our sins, although we can never put things right between us and God, we have someone who can. That's a tremendous encouragement. We're ashamed of our sin, we're ashamed that we do have to confess sin to our Saviour, but let us take comfort from his readiness and his ability to intercede with God effectively on our behalf.

There may be another person, who is anxious about sin, and has come to the conclusion that he or she is not able to do anything about it, to get rid of it, and doesn't know where to turn. What am I going to do? 'Iniquities, I must confess, / prevail against me do' (Psalm 65:3). I've got no righteousness. I have nothing I can say in my own defence. What am I to do? Where am I to go? Well, those who have an advocate would like to remind you that this advocate is accessible to sinners—that he receiveth sinners—that he takes on the worst of cases, that he's never turned anyone away because of the kind of people they were or because they were unable to pay for his services. The only thing a sinner who is anxious about his sins can do is to commit himself to Christ—appeal to him to take on the bad case, and to plead it before God. Many anxious sinners go on through long periods of anxiety and concern, just because they won't make use of the services, freely offered to them in the gospel, of an advocate with the Father, who's ready to plead the case of sinners.

Then there's the person who doesn't have an advocate, and who is not anxious about sins. Oh, perhaps occasionally, perhaps in certain situations, something comes to mind that makes the person afraid of eternity, afraid of judgment, because of sin. But it soon passes. It's not a real concern at all, it's just a passing concern. On the whole, this person is not anxious about sin. Well, when you think of what is necessary to secure the acquittal of a sinner, when you think of all that went behind the provision of an advocate with the Father, when you think of the eternal purposes of grace, when you think of the coming into this world of the Son of God in human nature, when you think of the perfection of his life and obedience, when you think of his death under the curse of God on the cross of Calvary, when you think of all that was required to put away sin, how sad is the condition of the person who's not concerned about sin, and who thinks it's something that can be dealt with in a moment, if it's got to be dealt with at all! The fact that there's an advocate with the Father, and that the only plea he can present is that he himself has borne the wrath of God in his own person—that fact should surely bring home to the careless sinner how dangerous that condition is. If only Christ by his death can take away sin, a few tears are not going to do it! A little amendment is not going to do it! A balancing out with better things is not going to do it! What a loud call to repentance—to face up to the fact of sin, to become concerned about sin—is found in this truth that's before us here! Yes, there's caution and there's comfort for the Lord's people, and there's encouragement for anxious sinners, but there's a solemn warning for those who are not afraid of sin, and not afraid of sinning, and not afraid of the wrath of God. Oh, think of what Christ suffered as the sin-bearer, so that he could take away the sins of his people! And ask that the Lord would bless that, to make you feel what an awful thing sin is, and what a dangerous thing it is to be bearing that burden alone, as one who travels towards the judgment seat of Christ.

May the Lord bless his Word.

8

Themes in 1 John
The marks of a true Christian

1 JOHN 2:3-6

And hereby we do know that we know him, if we keep his commandments. He that saith, I know him, and keepeth not his commandments, is a liar, and the truth is not in him. But whoso keepeth his word, in him verily is the love of God perfected: hereby know we that we are in him. He that saith he abideth in him ought himself also so to walk, even as he walked.

LORD'S DAY MORNING, 27TH APRIL 2008

We have been considering what is taught in the previous verses of this Epistle concerning the Scriptures, concerning God, concerning sin, and concerning the Saviour. And in these verses we have an account given of those sinners who are enabled to come to God, to come to know God, and to have fellowship with God, through the mediation of the Lord Jesus Christ. The questions arise, who are these blessed people? How are they known? What does it mean to be a Christian? How does being a Christian manifest itself to us and to others?

1. So as the Lord would enable us, the first thing we would consider is what it means to be a Christian, as that is set before us in these verses.

2. Then secondly, how a Christian is known—what is it that proves that a person is a Christian?

3. Then finally, the necessity of applying these tests to ourselves and to our own Christianity.

1. What does it mean to be a Christian?

First of all, what does it mean to be a Christian? It's obviously not just belonging in a general sort of way to the Christian religion. It's not just making a profession that one is a Christian. These are ways of speaking that are correct enough in their own place. But what is being brought out here is what a Christian really is—what kind of person is it who has the reality that's being professed when a person says 'I am a Christian'?

There are three things in these verses which bring out the reality of being a Christian. The first thing is, in verse 3, if we are Christians, we *know him*. 'Hereby we do know that we know him.' And then the next thing, in verse 5, if we are Christians we are *in him*. 'Hereby know we that we are in him.' And in verse 6, we *abide in him*. It's not a temporary, passing thing, but it's a permanent relationship. So these three things identify a Christian—we know him, we are in him, and we abide in him.

Now, to know God in Christ is a term which includes everything from the most elementary experience of God in a saving way, to the height of blessedness. *Knowing God* is included in the initial experiences of a person coming to see himself as a sinner and coming to rest on Christ for salvation. And *knowing God* is something that in its fulness will make heaven to be heaven to the Lord's people. The blessedness of heaven is just the perfect development of that initial acquaintance with God in Christ which a poor sinner has, when he casts himself or herself on the mercy of God in Christ Jesus.

'We know him.' We know the facts about him—or we know a little of them anyway—we've been confronted with the revelation which God has given of himself in Christ and which he has recorded in his Word. But through the facts we know about him, we have come to know himself. We've come to have a personal acquaintance with God, a personal relationship to God. We've been brought to acknowledge him as the God that he is. We have experienced something of his love drawing us to himself, and we have begun to love him in return. There's a relationship, there's an attitude, there's experience involved in knowing God. It goes beyond simply knowing about him—although we have to know about him before we can know him, we can know about him without knowing him. The Christian is the person who not only knows about God, but what God is has become a reality to that person, and that person has come to react to God in an appropriate manner.

That includes repentance for sin. It includes confidence in his mercy and in his faithfulness. It includes obedience to his revealed will. To know him, in this way, is to have one's life dominated by the existence of God in Christ. Nobody can know God without God becoming the preeminent force in that person's life. Some of the people we know become very prominent in our lives, while others that we've met in the passing, perhaps we can say that we know them, but they're on the periphery of our lives. But if we know God, he's at the very centre of our lives. If we know Christ, he has become everything to us, in the sense that we cannot do without him. We don't always feel like that. Some people may worry that they're not Christians, because Christ is not before their minds all the time, and they're not conscious of loving him all the time, or trusting him all the time. Well, is there anyone that can say that Christ is to them what he ought to be? But the fact is that, when it comes to the bit, that's where the soul gravitates toward—toward Christ. To whom can we go but unto thee? 'Thou hast the words of eternal life' (John 6:68).

To keep this 'knowing him' to the context, remember that last week we were thinking about Christ as our advocate with the Father and as the propitiation for our sins—the one who represents our case before God, and the one who bore the wrath that was due to us for our sins. Well, if we know him—if we know God in Christ—we come to God through the advocate, and we flee from the wrath to come to Christ. You see, we may have some strange notions of what knowing God means. But it's got a very practical aspect to it. If we know God, then to us he is holy and he is righteous, and we can only approach him through the Lord Jesus Christ. And if we know him, we've come to see that Christ is a suitable and sufficient advocate for us. And more or less consciously, more or less confidently, we are putting our case in his hands. And when we become conscious (as we do from time to time) of how exposed we are to the wrath of God, we don't try to hide underneath our own righteousnesses—we don't try to hide behind delusions about God and his universal love, and his readiness to compromise—but rather we flee to Christ to cover us. The only hope we have is that *he* is a hiding place. A man shall be as a hiding place for us (Isaiah 32:2). We know him. We know God in Christ, and therefore we cannot do without the advocate. And we cannot do without him as the propitiation for our sins. That's what it means to be a Christian—to be a person who knows God in Christ, in that practical and experimental as well as intellectual way.

The second way of describing what it means to be a Christian is by saying we are *in him*. This term speaks about the union which exists between God in Christ and his people. We are in him. It's very difficult to say what that means, because the concept of one person in another is something so alien to human experience. But this is a divine reality. Christ and his people maintain their distinct personalities, and will do so eternally. And yet, the union is so real and binding and intimate that a Christian is 'a man who is in Christ' (2 Corinthians 12:2)—who is so united to him that, although they are distinguishable, they are not separable. And when God looks at Christ, he sees all his people. And when he looks at one of his people, he sees Christ. They're so joined, that Christ was brought down to the experience of the awful curse of God against sinners in the place of his people—their union was so real, that when the sins of his people were attributed to him, imputed to him, he bore the full consequences. And the other way round—when a sinner is united to Christ, all the righteousness of Christ, all the achievements of Christ, are credited to him. He gets the benefit of them. 'A man in Christ.' Drawing out of the fulness that's in Christ. Depending on Christ. Somebody said it suggests that we are wrapped round by his divine perfections. He has taken us into his mind, he has taken us into his heart. A Christian is not a person who has some remote connection with the Lord Jesus Christ, but a person whose life and destiny are bound up with the Saviour.

And finally the third thing it says by way of describing what it means to be a Christian is that we *abide in him*. This is a relationship that lasts—to know him, to be in him, and to abide in him. It's an ongoing relationship—we're as dependent on Christ at the end as at the beginning. It's like the vine and the branches. Cut off the branches, and it's not going to bring forth fruit—it will soon wither and die. But abiding in the vine, remaining connected to that source of life, it will grow and it will bring forth fruit. That's what is true of the person who is a Christian. Once a Christian, always a Christian. Once in Christ, always in Christ. There's a persevering element in faith because faith is the means of the power of God operating— 'kept by the power of God through faith' (1 Peter 1:5). It's as if the power of God is flowing through faith, keeping faith alive, enabling the believer to persevere in believing. So a Christian is a person who's persevering in believing, persevering in drawing out of the fulness that is in Christ Jesus. It's a God-centred, Christ-centred life.

So to be a Christian is to know him, to be in him, and to be abiding him. What a glorious privilege—to be so related! 'A people near unto him,' the psalmist said (Psalm 148:14). A people near to him—could we be nearer to him than being *in him*? 'Your life is hid with Christ in God' (Colossians 3:3). So it's not a little thing, to be a Christian. It's not just making a decision—not just having a certain outward kind of life—but it's having a very personal, deep, abiding relationship with God as he has revealed himself in Jesus Christ.

2. How is it known that a person is a Christian?

Well then, how do we know—what is it that proves that a person is a Christian?

We don't normally have to ask for evidence that we know a person—we either know them or we don't know them. We wouldn't normally have to work out in our own minds, 'Do I really know this person or not?' We either know him or her, or we don't.

But this is spiritual, and we do not walk by sight, but by faith. And there's so much corruption in our own hearts, there are so many temptations from the devil, that it's not always the cut and dried thing that people think it is. Do I know him, or not? Some people have a strong assurance. Some people know that they are not Christians.

And some people don't know whether they are Christians or not. And that's one of the main reasons why this Epistle was written—so that those who are Christians would *know* that they are Christians—so that those who are the Lord's people, those who are believers, would *know*—so that they would have assurance. A person *can* know, and a person who is a Christian can't rest *without* knowing. There are no doubt times when we just go on from day to day, but when we come to our senses, we're really concerned—'Am I his, or am I not? Am I really a child of God?'

The means of knowing this have been provided. Of course, the Spirit is the great witness. We need the work of the Holy Spirit to assure us of God's love, to assure us that we are in Jesus Christ. But the Spirit works through means, and the apostle again mentions three things that indicate that a person does know him, is in him, is abiding in him. First of all, if a person keeps his commandments (verse 3). And secondly, if a person keeps his Word (verse 5). And thirdly, if a person walks even as he walked (verse 6). These are things that prove that a person really is a child of God.

First of all, we know that we know him *if we keep his commandments*. 'Ye are my friends, if ye do whatsoever I command you' (John 15:14). 'If ye love me, keep my commandments' (John 14:15). 'This is the love of God, that we keep his commandments: and his commandments are not grievous' (1 John 5:3). I think that's a very helpful expression that John uses—we keep his commandments, and his commandments are not grievous. 'O how love I thy law!' (Psalm 119:97). What *is* grievous is our disobedience—what *is* grievous is our inability to keep the commandments—but the commandments themselves are not grievous to us. We wish we *could* keep them—we wish we *could* walk according to them. 'Hereby we do know that we know him, if we keep his commandments.'

Knowing God results in keeping the commandments—it has these moral consequences. Experience of grace becomes manifest in the practice. You can see that, when you think of what it means to believe in the Lord Jesus Christ—it's to rest on him as a Saviour from sin. 'Thou shalt call his name Jesus: for he shall save his people from their sins' (Matthew 1:21). If we're trusting in Christ to save us from sin, the natural, logical consequence will be that sin will be something we want to be delivered from, and we will be desiring to keep the commandments of God. If we know him, we will keep his commandments, because the very purpose we have in coming to know him is to be made holy—to be delivered from the love and power of sin.

And also, there's the fact that if we know him, we have been given that knowledge by the Holy Spirit—it's the Holy Spirit who has given us faith in Christ. And the Holy Spirit's work is *one*. He doesn't give a person faith in Christ as a Saviour from sin—from the guilt of the sin—and not also give that person a desire for holiness. The whole work is one. If he has done anything in us savingly, he has done everything in us savingly. He has made us look to God to deliver us both from sin's guilt, and also from sin's power. So, if we know him, we will keep his commandments, because our knowledge of him depends on the work of the Holy Spirit within us, which work is one, and part of that work is to make believers holy.

And then also, if we know him we will keep his commandments because our desire in knowing him is to be in communion with God, in conformity with God, who is light and who is love. And how can we wish to be in communion with God and to have conformity to God, without wishing to be obedient to his commandments? So it follows, logically, that to know him will result in keeping his commandments.

But of course, when we speak of keeping his commandments, we have to remember that this keeping is not a legalistic, self-righteous, self-saving keeping of the commandments of God. We're not keeping the commandments so that we can make that the basis of our hope for eternity. If the Lord's people have learned anything, they've learned that they can never keep the commandments in a way that will constitute a basis for their hope for eternity. They're not keeping the commandments so as to save themselves by their obedience. They're keeping the commandments from the heart—it's not something external, not something forced on them. They're willing to obey—it's a keeping that arises from the new nature that's within them. People can feel, 'Well, I better do this, or I better do that,' because they feel as if they're being hedged in. They want to throw off God's law and throw off these chains, but they think they'd better just conform—they know enough to realise that they had better just conform. Well, the Lord's people have an inner principle now that makes them *love* God's law, and their heart is in it, their will is in it. The keeping of the commandments is not just something forced on them, it's not just something external—it's an internal thing. Supposing there was nobody else to see them, supposing there was no outward expression to be given, they desire within their hearts to be conformed to the will of God.

But also, when we think of this keeping of the commandments, we have to remember that it's never something which allows us as to dispense with the services of Christ as our advocate and as our propitiation. The child of God's keeping of the commandments would bring him to hell, if that's what his hope for eternity was based on. The child of God is very conscious of that. And at the end of every day, looking back on the day that has gone, oh how they feel, in the very best endeavours that they've made, they've been sinning against God, and deserve nothing but his wrath and his curse! And how that drives them again and again to the fountain which is opened for sin and for uncleanness, to the perfect righteousness of the Redeemer! The keeping of the commandments which marks a person out as knowing God is far from perfect—it's so polluted by sin—that we need Christ as our advocate—the advocate for our *good* works, as well as our bad works. We need him for the propitiation for our sins, to turn away the wrath of God, which we deserve in ourselves, as much today as we ever did.

So this 'knowing God' finds expression in a keeping of the commandments which is genuine and hearty and comprehensive of all the commandments of God—a desire to be conformed to the Lord's will. And yet it's not the basis of their hope, and it never reaches a level which makes it unnecessary to seek mercy, to seek the advocacy of Christ, to shelter under the mercy seat, to have the wrath of God turned away from us in our best moments. I think that's what's grows on a person, as they go on in the Christian way. There was a time when there were certain things that they looked at in their lives which made them feel exposed to God's displeasure. But now they can't see anything that doesn't leave them exposed to God's displeasure. Their prayers and their preaching and their hearing and their good works—they're all so polluted by sin that they feel how much they need Christ, and yet they're longing to be holy, to be able to keep the commandments of God perfectly.

The second thing mentioned here which proves a person is a Christian is that *they keep his Word*. 'Whoso keepeth his word, in him verily is the love of God perfected: hereby know we that we are in him.' 'His Word' must be wider than merely his commandments—it must include whatever God has said, whatever God has revealed—the Scriptures of the Old Testament and of the New Testament. Every word of God is pure, and it's precious to the Lord's people. There are probably some parts of the Bible that they find more precious than others, that speak to them more than others do. We should really hear the voice of God in every part of Scripture, but there's no doubt that there are parts of Scripture that have meant more to some people at certain times than others have. But the whole Scripture, the whole truth of God, is inspired of God and it's all precious to his people.

And they keep it—they preserve it, they observe it, they guard it in their hearts and in their minds. They endeavour to obey it. There are words used about Herod, when he had John the Baptist in prison: he heard him, and observed him, and did many things (Mark 6:20). That 'observing' means that he was keeping him, he was preserving him from the doom that others wanted to bring on him. Observing or keeping here no doubt means that the Word of God is something very precious to those who are in Christ. It is something that they wish to preserve and to keep and to observe and to obey. You can tell a lot about a person, or a person can tell a lot about himself or herself, by their attitude to Scripture.

When someone keeps God's Word, 'in him verily is the love of God perfected.' Truly, the love of God is perfected in the person who keeps his Word—it accomplishes its end. The love of God toward his people produces love in them toward him, and the outcome of that is that that person keeps the Word of God. The

Word of God is precious to the person who loves God, because God first loved him. You can't love God and despise his Word. This is why this is one of the marks that are brought forward to encourage people to believe that God has worked a work in them. If we love God whom we have not seen, we will love his Word which we have seen. This is his communication to us. This is the means of our knowledge of him. Take that Word away, and we have nothing. We've nothing to build on for eternity. This Word of thine is the ground of my sure hope, it's my comfort in my affliction, it's a lamp and a light, it's all I have to guide me to eternity, to guide me to God, to guide me to Christ! If we are in Christ, if the love of Christ is in us, if we love God who first loved us, then we'll have a regard for his holy Word.

And the third thing here which proves a person is a Christian is that they will *walk even as he walked*. 'He that saith he abideth in him ought himself also so to walk, even as he walked.' That must refer to the walk of Christ in this world. He was God manifest in the flesh. If we want to see what it means for a person who is God and who is perfectly conformed to God to walk in keeping with God, we have to look to Christ, who is holy, harmless, undefiled, and separate from sinners (Hebrews 7:26).

Saying 'he walked' refers to the course of his life. It's not isolated incidents, but the general tenor of a people's lives that tells whether they are Christians or not. Yes, they have falls, they stumble, and they wander out of the way, and they go into what Bunyan calls by-path meadows, and they don't make progress as they ought to do. But the general tenor of their life is toward the things of God—toward God, toward Christ. And they come back again—they're brought back again. Although they fall, they rise again. Although they go to sleep in by-path meadow, they wake up again and they set out on the way.

This desire they have for God and for obedience is the predominant principle in their lives. And that's what we should be testing. You see, when we just concentrate on particular moments in life, we can become either fearfully depressed or wrongfully elated. But what we have to ask is, 'What is the direction in which I am going? Am I walking as he walked?' Christ walked with God as no one else ever did. Are we walking as he did, desiring God, desiring holiness, desiring the honour of God? That's the question. If I'm in him, then I must be walking as he walked. The tenor of life, the course of life, the direction of life, will be in the same direction as the life of Christ himself. Oh, we feel so far away from that. But we mustn't close our eyes to reality. However far away we are from it, are we walking as he walked? Are we pressing toward the mark, for the prize of the high calling of God in Christ Jesus? (Philippians 3:14).

These are the sort of things that prove that a person is a Christian. They keep the commandments, admittedly in that imperfect way which means they're as dependent on Christ as they ever were, but they keep them from the heart. This is their endeavour. As usual, the Catechism puts it so well: 'full purpose of, and endeavour after, new obedience'. And they keep his word. 'Thy word have I hid in my heart' (Psalm 119:11). They wish they could remember it better than they do, but they desire to love it and to preserve it and to walk according to it. And they walk as he walked. Whatever deviations, whatever falls, whatever setbacks, the course of life is aiming in the same direction as Christ was aiming at—the glory of God, the enjoyment of God, the perfect obedience to the will of God.

3. Applying these tests to ourselves

Finally, we have to apply these tests to ourselves. Sadly, as the apostle points out here, there are those who say that they know him, and do not have these evidences. So they're really just telling lies, and the truth is not in them. 'He that saith, I know him, and keepeth not his commandments, is a liar, and the truth is not in him. But whoso keepeth his word, in him verily is the love of God perfected.'

These marks are given in order to be applied. We have to apply them to ourselves, and we have to ask the Lord to apply them to us, to examine us and to search us. That's something that we find the Lord himself doing in his ministry on earth—he brought before people the need to make sure that they are right in their relationship to God. In the sermon on the mount, for example, we find him saying, 'Not every one that saith unto me, Lord, Lord, shall enter into the kingdom of heaven; but he that doeth the will of my Father which is in heaven. Many will say to me in that day, Lord, Lord, have we not prophesied in thy name? and in thy name have cast out devils? and in thy name done many wonderful works? And then will I profess unto them, I never knew you: depart from me, ye that work iniquity' (Matthew 7:21-23).

You see, it's not what we *say*—it's not even how we *feel*. The standard in the judgment, the test that will be applied in the judgment, is what we *do*. And the test that will be applied in the judgment is the test that we should be applying while we're here. I think it was Jonathan Edwards who said that we should weigh ourselves in the scales that will be used to weigh us in the day of judgment. There's no use weighing ourselves in scales that are set to give a good impression of us here and now—we have to weigh ourselves in the scales that will be used by God in the day of judgment. God is not going to assess us by what we said about ourselves, and he's not going to assess us by how we felt about ourselves. He is going to assess us by what evidence there was in our lives that we really knew him, and were in him, and were abiding in him.

And the test will be what we've just been considering. Did we keep his commandments? Did we keep his Word? Did we walk as he walked? You remember in the 50th Psalm, the Lord was saying that there are people who take his covenant in their mouths, but they cast his words behind their back. That's a vivid representation of the sad reality—people saying the right things, feeling quite good concerning themselves—but throwing his words behind their back, not paying attention to the Word of God, not living according to the Word of God. 'How dare you,' he says, 'take my covenant in your mouth?' Again there is something similar in Psalm 26. There has to be integrity, there has to be conformity to the will of God, to prove the reality of one's devotion to God. That's why the psalmist was asking God to examine him and to prove him. In Psalm 139 we also have the same appeal to God. 'Examine me, and do me prove. Search into the very innermost parts of my soul, and if there's a wicked way in me, reveal it, and lead me in the way everlasting. If I'm not right, then show me.' Sometimes it's something that's very difficult to ask the Lord to do—to examine us. There might be times when we can say fairly easily, 'Examine me, and do me prove; / try heart and reins, O God.' But when we think about it, when we think about ourselves, and the little we know of our own sinfulness, it perhaps makes us hesitate. But we have to keep going. We have to ask him. We have to submit to the searching light of his Word. We have to face up to the truth concerning ourselves, and we had better find it out in this world than in the world to come. It must be a terrible thing to go to eternity under a delusion. To go to eternity expecting to wake up in heaven, and we wake up in hell, must be a fearful, fearful thing.

But on the other hand, you see, some of the Lord's people, they can't say that they know him. They can't *say* that they know him, and they don't *feel* that they know him. But they *do* know him. And what reveals that is their life and conversation—the direction in which their thoughts are going, and in which their lives are going. That's what makes this not simply a warning against delusion, but also an encouragement to assurance. The fact is that, where these evidences exist, the reality exists. If we keep his commandments, if we keep his Word, if we walk as he walked, even with all the imperfection attached to our walk, and if we're kept coming back to the advocate, to the propitiation, to Christ—what an evidence is there that we *do* know him, we *are* in him, we *are* abiding in him!

The great test of the reality of faith is the practice that springs from the experience that we have. We're not good judges of ourselves. We either judge ourselves too harshly or too lightly. But we have to seek to apply the biblical tests, and we have to ask the Holy Spirit to apply these biblical tests to us—so that we're not left to our own reasoning. You remember what we have in John 3, where believers and unbelievers are distinguished. 'He that believeth on him is not condemned: but he that believeth not is condemned already, because he hath not believed in the name of the only begotten Son of God. And this is the condemnation, that light is come into the world, and men loved darkness rather than light, because their deeds were evil. For every one that doeth evil hateth the light, neither cometh to the light, lest his deeds should be reproved. But he that doeth truth cometh to the light, that his deeds may be made manifest, that they are wrought in God.' There are some creatures that are at home in the dark, and when light comes they scurry away into their holes. And there are others, and they work while it is day, and they go to bed at night, in the darkness. This is like the difference between those have grace in their hearts and those who don't. Those who don't have grace love the darkness, they don't want to face up to the truth about themselves. But those who have grace *want* to know the truth about themselves, they *want* to be walking in the day, they *want* to have things cleared up between themselves and God.

Well, we have matter here for self-examination, and we ought to be concerned to apply biblical rules—not rules that are different from the Scriptures so that the righteous are condemned and the unrighteous are acquitted. It's possible to test ourselves in a way that makes us come to a wrong conclusion on the one side or the other— either to think well of ourselves when we shouldn't, or to think ill of ourselves when we shouldn't. So we need divine guidance and divine help, to keep to just the tests the Bible prescribes. What is our attitude to Christ? What is our attitude to the commandments of God? What is our attitude to the Word of God? And in the light of these things, 'Examine me, and do me prove; / try heart and reins, O God: / for thy love is before mine eyes, thy truth's paths I have trod' (Psalm 26:2-3).

And there's also encouragement here. And that was really the reason that the apostle had, as he tells us, for writing the Epistle—it's so that Christian people would enjoy the assurance of their salvation. Assurance of salvation is something that's possible. It's something that's desirable. It's something that's in the gift of God. But it's something that he tells us we should be seeking in the way appointed. We should be seeking to be assured of our interest in the Saviour, to be able to say, 'We know that we know him. We know that we are in him. We know that we are abiding in him.' And one of the ways that the Lord uses to give that assurance—one of the ordinary means that he uses—is the applying of this rule, 'What is my attitude to his

Word? To his commandments? What is my attitude to himself? Am I endeavouring to keep all his commandments? And yet, am I going constantly, as if I hadn't kept any of them, to that fountain which is open for sin and for uncleanness, to the advocate, to the propitiation for sin?'

May the Lord bless his Word.

9

Warrants to believe

God's hearty invitation

Isaiah 55:1-5

Ho, every one that thirsteth, come ye to the waters, and he that hath no money; come ye, buy, and eat; yea, come, buy wine and milk without money and without price. Wherefore do ye spend money for that which is not bread? and your labour for that which satisfieth not? hearken diligently unto me, and eat ye that which is good, and let your soul delight itself in fatness. Incline your ear, and come unto me: hear, and your soul shall live; and I will make an everlasting covenant with you, even the sure mercies of David. Behold, I have given him for a witness to the people, a leader and commander to the people. Behold, thou shalt call a nation that thou knowest not, and nations that knew not thee shall run unto thee because of the Lord thy God, and for the Holy One of Israel; for he hath glorified thee.

LORD'S DAY EVENING, 16ᵀᴴ NOVEMBER 2008

When I was trying to speak last Sabbath about repentance and faith, and the relation between them, I mentioned *The Practical Use of Saving Knowledge*, which is usually found bound up with *The Westminster Confession of Faith*. This little booklet draws our attention to four 'warrants' which sinners have for believing in Christ. The first of these warrants it describes as 'his hearty invitation'. And the example that it gives of God's hearty invitation to sinners is these first five verses of Isaiah 55.

We're all acquainted with the context in which these verses appear. In Isaiah 53 we have an amazing revelation concerning the Saviour who was to come, concerning the sacrifice which he was to offer to save his people from their sins. Chapter 53 includes one of the clearest statements in the Bible of a substitutionary atonement. 'All we like sheep have gone astray; we have turned every one to his own way; and the Lord hath laid on him the iniquity of us all.'

And then in chapter 54 we have an account of the salvation which comes to sinners through the Lord Jesus Christ. In particular it's expressed in the form of the covenant into which God brings his people, a covenant relationship. 'Thy maker is thine husband.' It speaks of how the Lord has called his people into that relationship, how he is faithful to that relationship, and how he will never abandon them. 'For a small moment have I forsaken thee; but with great mercies will I gather thee. In a little wrath I hid my face from thee for a moment; but with everlasting kindness will I have mercy on thee, saith the Lord thy Redeemer.' He says too that the covenant of his peace will never be removed.

And now in the 55th chapter, we have God addressing this hearty invitation to sinners to avail themselves of the salvation that has been procured for sinners by Jesus Christ. It wouldn't matter how beautiful the house of God's salvation was, if there was no way into it. What is brought to our attention here is that there *is* a way into this salvation. The Lord himself in these words is summoning sinners, even the most destitute sinners, to avail themselves of the provision that has been made.

1. Let us try to think, first of all, of those to whom this invitation is addressed.

2. And then secondly to think of the invitation itself and the promises that are attached to it.

3. And then finally to think of the one through whom the invitation and the promises are made effective—the one who is spoken about and spoken to in verses 4 and 5.

1. Those to whom the invitation is addressed

Well, the invitation is addressed to 'every one that thirsteth'. Sometimes there's a discussion about what condition of sinner that describes. It seems to describe, first of all, in a general way, every sinner who comes under the sound of the gospel. Every sinner who comes under the sound of the gospel is by nature destitute of what is necessary for spiritual life and wellbeing—destitute of righteousness, destitute of holiness, destitute of spiritual life, dead in trespasses and sins, lacking what is necessary in their relationship with God.

It's quite interesting that Dr Kennedy, in his sermon on verse 3, speaks about him that thirsteth as describing the *state* and not the *feeling* of the person—that is, describing the destitution, the lack, whether the person is conscious of it or not. What we have to remind ourselves of again and again is the fact that the gospel is addressed to sinners *as sinners*, not to conscious sinners who are sensible of their sin, and who are desiring salvation. 'God now commandeth all men everywhere to repent: because he has appointed a day, in which he will judge the world in righteousness' (Acts 17:30-31). It is obvious of course that there are many who are in that condition who have no desire for anything other than the condition in which they are—no desire for God, no desire for righteousness, no desire for holiness. As long as they continue in that condition, they will have no interest in the gospel. But that does not mean that they are relieved of the obligation to hear the gospel and to respond to the gospel. Every one that thirsteth, every person who comes under the sound of the gospel, is commanded to repent and is invited to believe in the Lord Jesus Christ.

Then, the one that thirsteth might be thought of as one who has a desire. Calvin speaks about ardent desire. As we said, there are some in that condition who have no interest in the gospel, no interest in salvation. There are others, and the Lord has awakened them to realise something of their need as sinners—that they don't have what they need, that they don't have a righteousness that will stand the scrutiny of God, that they don't have holiness, they don't have spiritual life, they can't do anything good, anything that is pleasing to

God. And there's a desire in their souls for salvation, a desire in their souls for the forgiveness of their sins, for deliverance from this inability and helplessness and sinfulness that characterises them. There's a desire for Christ. We often think of the invitations of the gospel like this—they are addressed to every one in general who hears the gospel, but there's a sense in which, in these invitations, the Lord is putting his hand on the shoulder of the sinner who is conscious of sin and desiring salvation, and speaking in a very particular, personal way to that sinner.

So no one is excluded. And yet there is a special encouragement for the person who has become concerned about the state he's in, and is seeking after God.

Another thing about those addressed is, they have 'no money'. They have no means of acquiring what they need. They have no means of bargaining with God, they have no worthiness, they have nothing that they can bring to God in order to secure salvation from God. They're not only destitute of the things that they need, but they are destitute of the means of acquiring them.

That's not something we come to terms with very easily, because there's a bargaining spirit in us by nature, so that when we come to have some sense of our need, we try to present to ourselves and present to God something that will perhaps make our case more hopeful. We try to come to God with our tears, we try to come to God with our reformation, we try to come to God with our attempts at believing and repenting—as if this was a down payment which God would accept and grant us salvation. But we have no money. We have no currency that will be acceptable to God. And yet, the invitation is addressed to those who are in that condition. Not only are they lacking in salvation, but they have no means of remedying their situation.

Another thing we're told about them is that they are 'spending money for that which is not bread', and their 'labour for that which satisfieth not'. As far as having anything that can meet with God's approval is concerned, they have nothing. But whatever they do have, they are putting out in vain endeavours. Some of them are seeking satisfaction in earthly and material things. Sometimes even when people begin to be concerned in their consciences about their state, they try to get rid of these concerns by immersing themselves in what might be in themselves legitimate earthly activities—they do what they can to get rid of these concerns and these fears. But most people, without any concern, are occupied in trying to satisfy whatever cravings they have with the things of time and sense. What a futile endeavour! Like the man who said *to his soul*, 'thou hast much goods laid up for many years,' so you can sit back and enjoy yourself (Luke 12:19). He was trying to meet the needs of his soul from temporal, earthly, material sources.

But there's also an endeavour after life itself—after salvation—a labouring, which does not satisfy—seeking salvation by one's own endeavours, by one's own works. All ye that labour and are heavy laden You've got this burden of sin on you, and you're trying to get rid of it, but all your efforts, all your labour, is in vain.

So people come into these categories. These destitute souls— some of them have no sense of destitution; others are seeking a supply for their soul's need. They have no money, they have no means of acquiring that which they need. And yet, some are busy occupying themselves with the things of this world, as if these things could meet the demands of a soul that will never die. And other people are busily seeking after salvation by their own efforts, efforts which are in vain.

These are the people to whom the invitation, the hearty invitation of God, is addressed in these words. These are the ways in which they are described—thirsty, penniless, and engaged in futile endeavour. No doubt that covers all of us, one way or another, if we are strangers to Christ.

2. The invitation and the promises attached to it

Now the second thing, and no doubt it's the main thing, is the call—the invitation—and the promises which are attached to that invitation.

It's very much an invitation, a call, to listen to the Word of God. Even the word 'ho' is a summons to pay attention. People are passing by—they're passing by the gospel, they're passing by the way of salvation that is set forth in that gospel—and God is sounding this alarm, as it were—he's issuing this summons, 'Ho, every one that thirsteth.' 'Listen to what I have to say!' That is what God is saying by that word 'ho.' Because we're not listening to what God says, by nature. Even when we've become concerned about our souls, we don't listen to what God has to say. We have our own ideas, which we follow out until we find just how futile they are.

And that summons to listen continues throughout these verses. 'Hearken diligently unto me.' 'Apply your mind, apply your soul, to what I have to say to you,' God is saying. This is not something to be casual about. This is not something just to let in one ear and out the other. This is something that demands our attention. It's more important than anything else that we will ever hear, however long we live. The summons from God is to pay attention to the gospel. Hearken diligently! Put your mind into it, put your heart into it, put your soul into it!

'Incline your ear!' There's this element of determining to listen, choosing to listen, applying ourselves to listen to what God has to say. We must make it our business to listen to what God has to say.

'Hear, and your soul shall live.' Ho, hearken diligently, incline your ear, hear! This is a call, a summons, an invitation. God has spoken. God is speaking words of mercy. God is intimating the means whereby a sinner can come into possession of life that shall never end. And God is summoning us to listen to what he has to say—to obey the gospel, to bow to its authority, to believe the testimony that God gives.

And when one does listen, what strikes one about this invitation is that it's very much a call to *come*. It says, 'Ho, every one that thirsteth, *come* ye to the waters, and he that hath no money, *come* ye, buy and eat, yea, *come*, buy wine and milk, without money and without price. Incline your ear and *come* unto me.' In these three verses, four times the Lord is saying, 'Come.'

That's an amazing word from the mouth of God, addressed to sinners. We should expect him to have said, 'Depart from me.' That's the voice of divine justice. That's the voice that is echoed in our own conscience. That's the concern that sinners have when they do become anxious about their souls. 'How can God ever receive the like of me? How can I ever expect to get a welcome from the God of heaven? How can I expect to hear anything, now or in the day of judgment, but, "Depart from me, ye cursed, into everlasting fire, prepared for the devil and his angels"?' And that's what sinners will hear eventually. And it would be a terrible thing if any sinner was to go from under the sound of the everlasting gospel in this place to hear that word from the mouth of God the Son at last, 'Depart from me.'

But that's not what we're hearing today. The gospel is saying, 'Come, come, come, come!' It's a welcoming sound, the gospel of the grace of God. 'This man receiveth sinners, and eateth with them' (Luke 15:2). This man doesn't slam the door in the face of the beggar who comes with nothing but sin and misery to seek mercy. The door is open. The invitation is given. The encouragement is given. The call is given. 'Come! Come unto me!'

And then, how are we going to come? 'Well,' he says, 'although you've no money, come, buy and eat; yea, come, buy wine and milk without money and without price. Come and buy. Come and buy what you need. Buy it without money, and buy it without price.' It's quite interesting what two of the great preachers of the past have to say in the way of explaining how you can buy without money. Spurgeon says that buying was desiring to have something, and then agreeing to the terms on which you can have it, and then taking it for yourself. And he said, 'That's a transaction which makes what you obtain as surely your own as if you had paid for it yourself.' Desiring it, agreeing to the terms on which it is offered to you, and taking it to yourself.

John Kennedy also speaks about buying without money. He says it's by entering into debt that one buys without money. Entering into debt to Christ. Taking what he is freely offering to us in the gospel, and charging it to Christ's account. Buy without money and without price. 'Oh,' you're saying, 'I have nothing to bring.' Well, if we only believed that—if we were only brought to an end of ourselves and our own self-righteous endeavours—and made content to go into eternal debt to Christ—to receive what he purchased at a great price, to receive it free to us, without money and without price.

That's the invitation. Come and buy without money and without price. Come and take what is freely offered in the gospel of the grace of God.

And then, 'Eat.' Buy it, and then eat it. Partake of what is set before you in the gospel. 'Eat ye that which is good, and let your soul delight itself in fatness.' Come to the waters. Buy wine and milk. Buy this bread, and eat it. Partake of the provision which has been made in the everlasting gospel. The work of faith is described in various ways in the Bible, but this is one of the ways that the Lord Jesus Christ himself spoke of the work of faith—'You have to eat my flesh and drink my blood' (John 6:53). It's the personal appropriating—taking to oneself—actually making use of what is provided in the gospel. That's what we're called to do. Not to admire it, not to sit and look at it, but to actually take it and receive Christ, and what is in Christ for us.

And see how this invitation is accompanied by promises, some of them implicit and some of them explicit. You're thirsting. Well, here are waters—a river of water of life, proceeding from the throne of God and of the Lamb (Revelation 22:1). You don't need to die for thirst, when this river of the water of life is flowing past you. And everything you need is there. Christ is made unto us wisdom and righteousness and sanctification and redemption (1 Corinthians 1:30). Everything we need is in Christ. You can't think of anything that you need as a sinner in relation to God, but it has been provided in Jesus Christ, God's Son. And the clear message of the text is that if the thirsty soul will come and receive what is provided in the gospel, then that soul will be fully satisfied.

It speaks about waters, it speaks about wine, it speaks about milk, it speaks about bread. All that is good and necessary and wholesome and health-giving and delightful is to be found in Jesus Christ. It's not just the bare necessities, as it were. We're thankful for the bare necessities of salvation. It would be a wonderful thing to get to heaven even by the skin of our teeth. But that's not what is offered in the gospel to sinners who believe in Jesus. There's a fulness in Christ. It pleased the Father that in him should all fulness dwell. The fulness of the Godhead dwells in him bodily. He's full of grace and truth. And of his fulness have all we received, and grace for grace. Grace upon grace, a stream of grace, flowing from the fulness that is in Jesus Christ.

You see, we may just be living on a crumb at a time. We have our daily rations, and they seem very small at times. But they come from this fulness. That little strengthening that helps you just to keep going from day to day, that keeps your head from sinking below the flood, that comes from the fulness of strength that's in God. The power of Christ is resting on us. It doesn't mean we'll feel powerful. The apostle didn't feel powerful. 'When I am weak, then am I strong' (2 Corinthians 12:10). But behind that little strength that was keeping him going, there was the infinite strength of Jehovah. And it's the same with every aspect of this salvation that we can possibly think about. Our present taste of it, our present experience of it may be very small. But there's infinite resources behind it—enough to keep us going to all eternity.

And the thing about heaven—one of the differences between the regular experience of the Lord's people in heaven and our common experience on earth—is that in heaven we'll be able to enjoy to the fulness of our capacity. We won't just have enough to keep us going from day to day, but enough to fill us with joy that is unspeakable and full of glory. But it's that same fountain of life that's there to meet the need of the thirsty sinner who comes to Christ to drink from the waters. Christ said, 'If you knew who I was, you would have asked of me, and I would have given thee living waters, a fountain of living waters springing up to life eternal, a well that'll never run dry, so that you'll never thirst again' (John 4:10, 14). You'll always have a desire, but that desire will always be fully satisfied. Again that's a difference between earth and heaven. On earth we have our desires, and our desires get a little satisfaction, and we're left dissatisfied. But when the Lord's people get to heaven, they'll be desiring more than ever what's in Christ, but they'll have it to the full, and they'll never be dissatisfied. Always wanting more and yet never dissatisfied! But it's the same provision that the poor thirsty soul gets when they come to Christ. They eat what is good, and their soul delights itself in the fatness, the fulness, the sufficiency, the suitability that's in Christ.

Then the figure of eating and drinking is set aside when we come to verse 3, where it says, 'Hear, and your soul shall live; and I will make an everlasting covenant with you, even the sure mercies of David.'

'Your soul shall live.' The provision in the gospel makes souls live. Water and bread and wine and milk may help to keep life going in a person who is alive, but they certainly can't create life where life does not exist. But that's what the gospel does. It's a gospel for those who are dead in trespasses and sins, and it makes the dead soul live. That's the change involved in becoming a Christian, becoming a believer in the Lord Jesus Christ. It's the difference between death and life. And then, that life is sustained. The same grace that brought the soul alive keeps the soul alive, and meets all the needs of that living soul. That soul will live for ever—enjoy eternal life, which is knowing God the Father and his Son Jesus Christ (John 17:3).

And then he says, 'I will make an everlasting covenant with you, even the sure mercies of David.' The sinner who comes to Christ is in covenant with God. God reveals to that sinner the fulness that's in the covenant, and out of that covenant fulness he meets the sinner's every need with the mercies of David. These are the mercies that were promised to David's greater Son and Lord, Jesus Christ. David himself recognised that the covenant was something that would survive after his death. 'He hath made with me an everlasting covenant, ordered in all things, and sure.' It was a covenant that was finding its fulfilment in Jesus Christ. What is promised to sinners who come to Christ in response to this call is that they will enter into the possession and the enjoyment of all those mercies promised to Christ in the everlasting covenant for his people. You see, the promise was made in eternity. We didn't exist in eternity, but the Son of God existed, and the promises were made to him, for himself and for his people.

What was promised to him is described here as 'sure mercies'. All the provisions of the gospel of the grace of God—justification, adoption, sanctification, and all the benefits that flow from them, in this life, at death, and at the resurrection. All these things are sure mercies, because God has promised them and provides them—because Jesus Christ God's Son has procured them for his people, he met all the conditions—and because the Holy Spirit applies them to his people. That's how sure they are. That's how sure the salvation of the sinner who trusts in Christ is—they have the sure mercies of David, covenanted mercies. 'I will make an everlasting covenant with them,' as we have it in Jeremiah. The covenant was, 'I will not turn away from them, but I'll put my fear in their hearts so that they will not turn away from me' (Jeremiah 32:40). These are sure mercies. God will never abandon us, and we will never abandon God. Although we have in us an evil heart of unbelief, departing from the living God, the Lord will not allow his people to depart. The Lord holds on to them. They may wander, they may fall, they may go through very dark passages. But the Lord's everlasting arms are underneath them. His mercies are sure. They're bound up with Christ. Their life is hid with Christ in God (Colossians 3:3). How more secure could a person be than that? Your life is hid with Christ in God—is there anywhere more secure than in God and bound up with Christ in God?

These are the kinds of promises which accompany the invitation of the gospel to sinners. Thirsty, destitute sinners, stupid sinners who are trying to get salvation some other way, or who are trying to bury their heads in the sand and satisfy themselves with the things of this world. In spite of all your sinfulness and all your foolishness and all the futility of your endeavours, come to the waters, come and buy and eat, and you'll find the sure mercies of David. You'll be blessed with mercies that will never cease.

3. The invitation and the promises are made effective through Christ

The third thing we might just notice is the one through whom the invitation and the promises are made effective. All of this comes about because of what God says in verses 4 and 5. 'Behold, I have given him for a witness to the people, a leader and commander to the people. Behold, thou shalt call a nation that thou knowest not, and nations that knew not thee shall run unto thee because of the Lord thy God, and for the Holy One of Israel; for he hath glorified thee.'

First of all the Lord is speaking about him, in verse 4, and then he's speaking to him, in verse 5. It's David. 'The sure mercies of David—I have given him for a witness to the people.' But David was in his grave and had turned to corruption. So the David being spoken of here is the David of the New Testament, the Lord Jesus Christ. God is informing us here that these promises are given, and they'll be fulfilled, because he has given Christ to be a witness to the people, a leader and commander to the people.

He has *given* him. He sent his only begotten Son into the world in order to be and do everything that was necessary for the salvation of his people. He gave him to be a *witness*—a witness to God, to the holiness of God, to the grace of God—a witness by the words that he spoke, a witness by the life that he lived, but especially a witness by the death that he died. There's no greater testimony to the holiness of God and the justice of God and the grace of God than in the cross of our Lord Jesus Christ. That's where we see this prophetic work, this revelation of God, by Christ most clearly accomplished. He is also called a *leader*. He's the one who's going to lead sinners out of their state of sin and misery into a state of salvation by his power, by the word of his power accompanied by the Holy Spirit of God. He leads sinners, he draws them away from their sinful, lost state and puts them in possession of life. And he's a *commander*. He's brought them under the authority of God, and he exerts that authority over them, bringing every thought into captivity to the obedience of Christ.

And then God says to Christ, 'Behold, thou shalt call a nation that thou knowest not, and nations that knew not thee shall run unto thee because of the Lord thy God, and for the Holy One of Israel; for he hath glorified thee.' Here is the call of the gospel addressed to sinners. But are sinners going to come? That's the great predicament. The call is full and free. But where is the sinner who'll come to the Saviour? We won't come—not because of any insincerity in the call, but because of the corruption of our natures, the enmity of our mind against God, and our sinful inability. Well, he says to Christ, '*Thou* shalt call a nation that thou knowest not, and nations that knew not thee shall run unto thee.' There was no relationship, as it were, between the Saviour and these sinners—they did not know each other. But the Saviour's power is such that he calls them and they run. He sends forth his quickening Spirit, and they are persuaded and enabled to respond to his call. You see, this is the wonderful thing about the gospel. It's addressed to those who can't respond to it. But provision has been made for that—Christ has power through his Spirit to make his call effective and to draw sinners to himself.

And that, we are told, is 'because of the Lord his God, and for the Holy One of Israel'. God has given him that function. And it's for the glory of God that he performs that function. God is at the beginning and God is at the end of this work of salvation. He is the one who has provided the Saviour, and it is he who is glorified when the Saviour draws sinners through the gospel, through the power of his Spirit, to put their trust in him.

'For he hath glorified thee.' God glorified Christ, so that Christ would glorify God in the salvation of his people. You see that brought out in several places in John's Gospel, for example. It's interesting and profitable to consider how the Father glorified the Son—by exalting him to be the Saviour of his people—in order that the Son would glorify the Father, by finishing the work that the Father gave him to do. God has glorified Christ, exalted him to be a prince and a saviour, so that he will in that capacity draw sinners to himself, and bring them into the possession of the blessedness that has been described in these verses. 'I, if I be lifted up from the earth, will draw all men unto me' (John 12:32). He sends forth his Spirit and accompanies the call of the gospel with the power of his Spirit, and sinners run unto him. They were running away from him before. But when they hear the powerful voice that comes out from the Lord most high, they make for Christ. That's what shows that the call of the gospel has taken effect in the soul of a sinner. That sinner is making for Christ. They may be feeling far away, but that's the aim, that's the object. And that sinner will not rest until he or she comes to Christ—they'll not be able to stop short of Christ.

The question that we have to face is whether or not we have ever heard this call ourselves. We've heard often enough, since our earliest days perhaps, the invitation to come to the Saviour. But have we ever felt our own need of that invitation? And have we been brought to respond to that invitation and to come? Some people might say, 'Well, what's the point of asking people to come when they can't come?' But it's the same as when the Lord said to the man whose arm was withered, 'Stretch forth thy hand,' and he stretched it forth (Luke 6:10). There was a power accompanying the call, accompanying the command. He said to Lazarus in the grave, 'Come forth,' and he came forth (John 11:43). The call of the gospel says to sinners, 'Come to the waters.' And those who hear that call in their souls, they come to the waters. They come to Christ. They come to rest upon the provision that has been made in the everlasting covenant of God's grace. There's no safety, there's no security, short of Christ, short of this salvation.

Well, as I said at the beginning, this is what is spoken of as God's hearty invitation. This is God calling sinners—thirsting sinners, destitute sinners, with no means of remedying their situation—to come to Christ, and to find in Christ all their salvation, to find in Christ everything they need, for time and for eternity. God is saying, 'Ho, every one that thirsteth.' The voice of God is summoning us, once again, to listen to what he has to say, to listen to his voice, and to respond to that summons, and to come to the waters, and to drink abundantly. There's a fulness there, however destitute we are, however ill-deserving, however helpless. There's everything in Christ that a sinner will ever need.

May the Lord bless his Word.

10

Warrants to believe
God's earnest request

2 CORINTHIANS 5:18-21

And all things are of God, who hath reconciled us to himself by Jesus Christ, and hath given to us the ministry of reconciliation; to wit, that God was in Christ, reconciling the world unto himself, not imputing their trespasses unto them; and hath committed unto us the word of reconciliation. Now then we are ambassadors for Christ, as though God did beseech you by us: we pray you in Christ's stead, be ye reconciled to God. For he hath made him to be sin for us, who knew no sin; that we might be made the righteousness of God in him.

LORD'S DAY EVENING, 23RD NOVEMBER 2008

The first warrant for believing in Christ which is mentioned by the authors of *The Sum of Saving Knowledge* is his hearty invitation. The second warrant for believing in Christ is what they call 'God's earnest request to sinners to be reconciled to him in Jesus Christ.' That earnest request to which they're referring is to be found, as in many other places, in the verses before us here.

The apostle has been reflecting on himself as a Christian and as a Christian minister, and on how constrained he felt to press the gospel on sinners. He was constrained on the one hand by the terror of the Lord. When he thought of the judgment seat, when he thought of sinners hastening to the judgment seat of Christ, the terror of the Lord constrained him to persuade men—to be pleading with sinners to consider their latter end and to make use of the gospel.

But here is another side of what was constraining him, and that was the awareness he had of the reconciliation that God has provided for sinners in Christ, and the fact that God is calling sinners to enter in to that reconciliation—to enter in to a state of peace and harmony with himself through the Lord Jesus Christ. And that's what's brought to our attention here. We have reason to endeavour to speak concerning these matters as earnestly as we can, when we think on the one hand of the fact that we are making for the judgment seat and soon will stand together there, and on the other hand when we think of the fulness and the freeness of the gospel, and how the gospel is calling on sinners to avail themselves of this reconciliation that is in Christ for sinners.

　　1. The meaning of reconciliation
　　2. The means of reconciliation
　　3. The message of reconciliation.

1. The meaning of reconciliation

First of all, what is the meaning of reconciliation? Those who study etymology tell us that the original word comes from the idea of change or exchange, and particularly the change from enmity to friendship. That is basically what reconciliation between God and sinners is—where there was enmity before, there is friendship now.

When we think of the relationship between God and sinners, how different it is from that original relationship which we were trying to consider in the morning [sermon on Genesis 1:26-28], when God made man in his image and after his likeness, so that there could be perfect harmony and fellowship—so that God and men could walk together in peace. But the fall put an end to that. In the fall, all of us lost our right relationship with God, and instead of love for God and trust in God and obedience to God, there is enmity against God in the heart of every sinner. 'When we were *enemies*, we were reconciled' (Romans 5:10).

The sinner has no love for God. That is something we might find difficult to believe, until the Lord throws some light on the matter, because there are many people who don't think for one moment that there is anything in their hearts against God. That may even be the condition of many who come under the sound of the gospel. Yes, they know the doctrine which says that the carnal mind is enmity against God, but they're not conscious of any enmity themselves. They rather resent the suggestion that they hate God, that they have no confidence in God, and that they haven't got a spark of obedience in their souls or lives towards God. And yet that is the way with us. And it's when God becomes a reality to us, and when his law becomes a reality to us, that we discover the enmity that's in our hearts against him. That's how it was with the apostle Paul, as he brings out in Romans 7. He makes it very clear—he says, 'I was alive without the law once.' He felt he could hold up his head in the presence of God. He felt he was godly. He felt he was keeping the commandments—that if anyone could claim to be accepted on the grounds of his own works, it was him. But it was a different matter when the commandment came—when the law of God came home to his mind, to his heart, to his conscience, and it stirred up the sin that was within him, and it brought out the enmity that was in his heart against God. Then, he says, he died. He lost the view he had of himself. He discovered the reality of that doctrine which he was later to teach—the carnal mind is enmity against God. So that's one side of the matter. The sinner wants nothing to do with God—the sinner would like to be able to believe that God does not even exist, and the sinner lives as if God has no claim upon him.

But there's another side to this estrangement, to this alienation, to this variance between God and the sinner, and that is that God is angry with the wicked every day (Psalm 7:11). 'His soul hates the wicked man, / and him that violence loves,' because the righteous Lord loveth righteousness (Psalm 11:5, 7). The character of God, the nature of God is such, and the nature of sin is such, that God cannot look with favour on a sinner in his sin. He cannot have any friendly relationship with the sinner in his sin. The reality of God's displeasure, God's wrath against sinners, is something that's underlined in the Bible from the very beginning after the fall, right down to the last book of the Bible. Nothing is said more to the point concerning God's wrath than is said by Christ himself in the gospels. The very fact that Christ was on the cross of Calvary is a testimony to the fact that God is just and holy, and as such he cannot look with favour on anyone on whom sin lies. There is a breach—a breach has been made between God and men. Men are against God, and God is against men.

And that is the sad situation, the background against which alone we can understand the meaning of reconciliation in the Word of God. Because what that is bringing home to us is the fact that there is a way whereby that breach can be made up—a way whereby the quarrel between God and sinners can be made up—a way whereby harmony can be restored and friendship established where there was alienation and estrangement before.

The message of reconciliation is a message which proclaims that there is such a thing for sinners as peace with God, that it is possible for a sinner to walk with God, to be called the friend of God. Abraham was called the friend of God, and all the children of Abraham, all believers, are the friends of God. God is friendly disposed towards them. He has embraced them in his love and in his favour and in his fellowship, and they can draw near to God. They can make use of that friendship, they can come to him, believingly, prayerfully—they can come to him with all their sins and all their failures, all their concerns, all their troubles—because the old enmity has been destroyed, and now the love of God is shed abroad in the heart, and the sinner is no longer banished from God's presence.

So when we're thinking of reconciliation, we're thinking primarily of God being friendly disposed to the sinner, but the effect of that is the sinner becoming friendly disposed to God.

2. The means of reconciliation

Now, we have to notice that perhaps the main thing here is the means of reconciliation. How can it be that the breach can be mended, that God and the sinner can come together in friendship?

Of course, we have to notice that it all begins with God, and it is all accomplished by God. The initiative is not on the side of the sinner. No sinner would ever seek restored friendship with God. But 'all things,' we are told, 'are of God, who hath reconciled us to himself by Jesus Christ, and hath given to us the ministry of reconciliation.'

It's only God who *could* choose to establish this friendship. It's against God we have sinned. We are therefore justly exposed to his displeasure. We have no right to propose terms to God for the end of this warfare. And God is under no obligation to propose terms to us. But God in his sovereignty has chosen to establish harmony with sinners—to bring sinners back into fellowship with himself. God alone has the right, and God alone has the power, to do that. This expression, 'all things are of God,' is pointing to the fact that reconciliation originates with God. Both the message of reconciliation originates with God, and the capacity to receive the reconciliation originates with God—God making a sinner a new creature who's able to receive the terms of the gospel. It all begins with God. God is the reconciler.

It's not even as if Christ has risen up in order to establish peace between God and sinners. It is God who sent Christ to be the Saviour of sinners. '*God* so loved the world, that he gave his only begotten Son, that whosoever believeth on him should not perish, but have everlasting life' (John 3:16). 'Herein is love, not that we loved God, but that he loved us, and sent his Son to be the propitiation for our sins' (1 John 4:10). 'We love him, because he first loved us' (1 John 4:19). That is something that is fundamental in the teaching of the Bible. It all begins with God, with his sovereign good pleasure, with his sovereign grace, with his sovereign love.

But the Bible makes it very clear that God *could not*—and I hope we say it advisedly—God could not just bring himself and sinners together by a word, as he created all things by the word of his power. The nature of God, the holiness of God, the inflexible justice of God, on the one hand, and the nature of sin on the other hand (being an assault on the very being of God, on the holiness of God, on the right of God to reign) make it inevitable, make it necessary, that God would be angry with the sinner. The anger of God is not a 'passion,' such as is found in man—not something that can die out and pass away. It is a determination to punish sinners, a holy and righteous and necessary determination to punish sinners. 'Because the Lord most righteous doth / in righteousness delight' (Psalm 11:7) therefore 'they who are wicked into hell / each one shall turned be' (Psalm 9:17). 'Snares, fire and brimstone, furious storms, / on sinners he shall rain: / this, as the portion of their cup, / doth unto them pertain' (Psalm 11:6). The absolute necessity of sin being punished by a holy God is something that underlies the whole message of the gospel, the whole work of Christ. God would not have put Christ to the cross of Calvary if it wasn't necessary for the salvation of sinners. But the purpose of God to reconcile his people to himself meant that he had to find a way (if we can speak like that) whereby he could do that consistently with his own holy and righteous character.

No one but himself could devise such a way, but that is the way that's revealed to us in the gospel—the way that was formulated, if we can say that, in the everlasting covenant—that Christ and his people would be joined together so that he could act for them, and he could take on their liabilities. He could become accountable for them, represent them before the bar of the court of heaven, and take on all the implications of their alienation from God, and therefore relieve them of the burden of their sin and secure for them a perfect righteousness. And that's what's brought out in these verses. God in Christ was reconciling the world to himself. He laid the burden of his people's sin upon Christ and, as a consequence, he does not impute their trespasses to them, but they are regarded as righteous—and they are righteous—in the Saviour.

Now notice the person through whom God reconciles sinners to himself. He's described as 'him who knew no sin'. (We have to sort out the words of the verse in our minds—'he hath made him to be sin for us, who knew no sin' means that it's 'he who knew no sin' whom he has made to be sin for us.) This is the description of the one through whom reconciliation is to be brought to sinners. He knew no sin. He had no consciousness of sin, because he had no sin to be conscious of. That's the glory of Christ. He was holy, harmless, undefiled, and separate from sinners. There never was a holier person than him on the face of the earth. He is the holy God, and he is a perfectly holy man. He is a holy Redeemer—there is no sin in him, but positive obedience, positive conformity to the will of God in every matter. He could say to people, 'Which of you convinceth me of sin?' and they could say of him, 'I find no fault in him at all.' And one higher than them all could say, 'This is my beloved Son, in whom I am well pleased.'

Does that not show us that what he suffered and endured in his life, and particularly in his death, was not deserved by him? It was not on account of anything in himself personally. And it shows us how suitable he was to be a Saviour. He had nothing to answer for, for himself. All that he experienced was due to the sins of others. The great high priest *must* be holy and harmless and undefiled and separate from sinners—his obedience must be perfect. And that's what's written concerning Christ—that's what makes him such a suitable Saviour. He is God and man, and he is absolutely perfect as God and as man, and that qualifies him to represent others—he has nothing to answer for himself.

But then we see what was done to him—what the Lord did to him. He imputed to him the sins of his people. 'He hath made him to be sin for us.' He hath made him to be sin. What a way of emphasising how real and how thorough was the identification of the sins of his people with Jesus Christ! We couldn't think of a way of expressing just how responsible, how accountable, for the sins of his people Christ became, other than the way that the Holy Spirit has described it: 'He hath made him to be sin for us.' There wasn't a speck of sin on the person of Christ or in the nature of Christ. He continued through all his experience to be holy, harmless, undefiled, and separate from sinners. And yet, in his representative capacity, he bore all the sins of his people. And the consequences of these sins came upon him. 'All we like sheep have gone astray; we have turned every one to his own way; and the Lord hath laid on him the iniquity of us all' (Isaiah 53:6). He's the only holy one, and yet (as Smeaton said), there was never such an accumulation of sin on the head of anyone as there was on the head of Christ. He was the only holy one, and yet all the sins of all his people were laid to his account. And in his official character, as the representative of his people, he answered to God for these sins. And God said, 'Awake, O sword, against my shepherd, and against the man that is my fellow' (Zechariah 13:7). 'He was wounded for our transgressions, he was bruised for our iniquities: the chastisement of our peace was upon him; and with his stripes we are healed' (Isaiah 53:5). What we're seeing when we look at the cross of Calvary, and when we hear him saying, 'My God, my God, why hast thou forsaken me?' (Psalm 22:1) is the imputation to Christ of all the sins of all his people. He was made sin. He who was the very embodiment of holiness became the very embodiment of the sins of his people. And he was made a curse for us. The curse of God will always follow sin. And the curse of God followed sin when it was laid to Christ's account, and he was subjected to the reality of the wrath of God which would have destroyed the people of God eternally. This person had the sins of all his people laid to his account, and the curse due to them pursued him and was poured out on him to the uttermost. He drank the cup of their damnation till it was dry.

And then, you see, following on from that, God does not impute to them their trespasses, but they are made the righteousness of God in him. There's this counter-imputation, as it's called. Our sins were imputed to Christ, and his righteousness is imputed to his people. Their sins are not imputed to them any more—their trespasses, their false steps, their transgressions of God's law. He sees no iniquity in his people. There's nothing in them any more that he's going to pursue with his justice. Oh, they're the ones who're doing the sinning, and their sins bring them under God's displeasure, and the Lord will correct them for their sins and make them feel their sins and make them confess their sins, every day of their lives. But as far as bringing them into condemnation is concerned, as far as their dealings with the Judge is concerned, he does not impute their trespasses unto them. 'Not imputing their trespasses unto them.'

He treats them no longer as guilty sinners who deserve to perish, because Christ died. Christ paid the penalty in their place. It's something that couldn't happen in any other circumstances, in any other relationship, but it's something that could happen between Christ and his people. He has paid the price, paid the penalty, and now, as far as the Judge is concerned, they are set free. What a glorious truth that is for a poor sinner! Toplady wrote, 'Payment God will not twice demand, / first at my bleeding Surety's hand, / and then again at mine.' That's the truth that's set before us here. God would not be just if he was to punish those for whom Christ died. That's one of the things that brings home to us the particularity of redemption, that Christ didn't bear the sins of everyone. He bore the sins of his people. The sins of his people have been atoned for by the death of Christ, and therefore there is now no condemnation to those who are in Christ Jesus.

And it's not just that he does not impute their trespasses, that the sentence is passed 'not guilty' and they can go free. But 'they are made the righteousness of God in him.' This is the glorious position of believers. Not just free from the guilt of sin, but possessing a divine righteousness, the righteousness of God. A righteousness God has provided. A righteousness that God approves of. But especially, a righteousness which is divine because it's the righteousness of a divine person. The *Lord* is our righteousness (Jeremiah 23:6). Jesus Christ is God, and the righteousness that he has wrought out for his people is the righteousness of God. And we are made the righteousness of God *in him*. Those who were guilty and ruined sinners in themselves, in the eyes of God are now as righteous as Christ is, because their righteousness is Christ's righteousness. It's not a human righteousness we have. That wouldn't do us much good, in the face of all that's against us. But it's a divine righteousness, and therefore a righteousness that will never cease to exist and will never cease to satisfy God. The poor Christian is often cast down because of trespasses and sins—and indeed we have much reason to be cast down because of our trespasses and sins. But here is something to counterbalance that. Here is something to lift us up when we're cast down—that in and through the Lord Jesus Christ, we have a righteousness which is divine, and which is therefore infinite and eternal and unchangeable. That's much better than what we lost when Adam fell.

And it's on that basis that sinners are reconciled to God—on the basis of sin not imputed, and on the basis of being righteous with the righteousness of Christ. I've mentioned before, and you've probably read, William Cunningham's words concerning 'the righteousness which God's righteousness requires him to require.' God cannot be satisfied with any righteousness other than that which meets all the demands of his righteousness, and that's what he has provided for his people in Christ. And if we're in Christ, we have there the basis of a friendship which will never again be broken up.

For whom then has this been provided? We're thinking about the means of reconciliation—the person of Christ bearing the sins of his people, securing deliverance from the guilt of sin, securing a perfect righteousness for them. And the question arises, 'Who are the beneficiaries of this reconciling work?' It says, 'God was in Christ, reconciling *the world* to himself,' and then it goes on to say, 'he hath made him to be sin *for us*, that we might be made the righteousness of God in him.'

Now obviously, according to the Bible, not every sinner on earth is reconciled to God. Not every sinner on earth has his trespasses not imputed to him. Not every sinner on earth is made the righteousness of God. There's no universal salvation, there's no universal atonement. The very idea of atonement (in the Bible certainly) excludes such an idea, because there's a personal relationship between the sinner who benefits from Christ's work and Christ himself. Satisfaction is given for specific sins. Substitution is made for specific persons. The terms 'for us' and 'in him' bring that fact before us. It's the person who's *in Christ* who is the beneficiary of this work of Christ and this reconciliation. It's those who are in Christ in the everlasting covenant, and in Christ by faith, united to the Saviour through believing. And when it speaks about 'the world', I think what Benjamin Warfield, the American theologian, said is true, that the universality that is spoken of here is opposed to the nationalism of the Jewish race—it is not opposed to the particularity of redemption. The apostle is pointing out that this is not just for the Jews, this is for sinners of mankind—this is for sinners everywhere, anywhere. Any sinner that will avail himself of this provision will enter in to the enjoyment of this blessedness. There's a generality in the proclamation of the gospel. 'Unto you, O men, I call'—any man, any human being, any sinner, anywhere, can be told that in Christ is a suitable Saviour, and be called to come to that Saviour. But additionally, 'the world' is also a term that brings out the kind of people, the character of sinners who are saved by Christ. 'Behold the Lamb of God, which taketh away the sin of *the world*'—the sin which characterises the world, the sin that is *our* sin. The worst sins of all are included in that, whatever they may be. It's telling us that this reconciliation is for the chief of sinners, the worst of sinners, the most stubborn of sinners, for sinners of mankind. Christ died for the ungodly. While we were enemies, without strength, without God, without hope. It's a gospel for sinners, *as* sinners.

3. The message of reconciliation

And that brings us just to notice the message of reconciliation. God has given unto us the ministry of reconciliation. He has committed unto us the word of reconciliation. 'Now then we are ambassadors for Christ, as though God did beseech you by us: we pray you in Christ's stead, be ye reconciled to God.'

You see, God in his Word tells us that this thing was not done in a corner. He commissioned his apostles and the Church to go into all the world and to preach the gospel to every creature. He has appointed ambassadors to represent him and to convey his message to sinners of mankind. In Greek, the word 'ambassador' is very similar to the word 'presbyter,' and seemingly the idea was that persons who had some experience of the court were sent out to represent the authority. Paul, for example, was one who had tasted that the Lord was gracious. He had experience of the grace of God. He could say, 'This is a faithful saying, and worthy of all acceptation, that Christ Jesus came into the world to save sinners; of whom I am chief' (1 Timothy 1:15). He knew what he was talking about, because he had experienced the grace of God—but he was sent forth, not to talk about himself, and not to make up the message himself, but to convey the message that God had given him.

That is the function of the ambassadors. God sets people apart, he calls them, he sends them, in order to convey as best they can, depending on his Spirit, the truth of his Word. That's why the Bible is open in front of us. You don't have to believe if you don't see it in the Bible. That is something that even in the most orthodox of churches we have to remember—what's said in the pulpit has to be tested by the Bible. We should be prepared to have what we endeavour to say tested in that way, because we should be endeavouring to communicate the message which God has given.

And when that message is communicated, the hearer has to do, not with the preacher, but with the one who sent the message, the one who sent the messenger. There's an authority in the Word of God, and that's what we have to deal with. It's not that this person said this, and that person said that, but, 'What says the Word of God?' That's what gives the efforts at preaching whatever authority they have—when it's what is written in the Bible. We are ambassadors for Christ, as though *God* did beseech you by us. We pray you in *Christ's* stead. What a solemn, crushing thought for those who endeavour to speak in the Lord's name, if it wasn't that the Lord sustained them, to think of the solemn responsibility of standing up and saying, 'Thus saith the Lord'! And how that should affect the hearing! As Paul said to those in Thessalonica, 'Ye received it not as the word of men, but as it is in truth, the word of God, which effectually worketh also in you that believe' (1 Thessalonians 2:13).

There's nothing divine about the preacher, but there's something divine about the message. And the message is not coming with the authority of Paul as a man, or any other man, but with the authority of God: 'in Christ's stead, as though God did beseech you by us' It makes the relationship between the pulpit and the pew a very solemn relationship. And it makes us thankful that God has sent sinners like ourselves to preach the gospel, not angels. What does an angel know about sin? What does an angel know about salvation? What does an angel know about trusting in the blood of Christ? No doubt they could speak with the tongues of angels, they could speak in a wonderful way about these things. But a person could say, 'What do you know about that? All you know is what you've heard and seen.' But God has chosen to take sinners, lost, ruined sinners, like Saul of Tarsus and like every other preacher since, and to use them, with all their sinfulness and weakness and failures, to try to communicate the truth of God as a truth which they've experienced themselves, so that they can say to sinners, 'Come thou with us, and we will do thee good: for the Lord hath spoken good concerning Israel' (Numbers 10:29).

And you notice that the message is communicated with the heart as well as with the head. 'We beseech you, we pray you, in Christ's stead.' As if Christ himself was beseeching you and praying you, begging you, to put your trust in him. It's a great cause of grief to us, how cold our hearts can be when we're speaking about the things of eternity and the things of God to our fellow sinners. If only we could get something of the spirit the apostle had, to be yearning over sinners, and pleading with them, and beseeching them to come to the Saviour. Why will you not come to Christ? Why will ye die? Samuel Rutherford had that spirit when he said, 'O, if one soul from Anwoth meet me at God's right hand, my heaven will be two heavens in Immanuel's land.' Paul was full of that spirit. He didn't want to go to heaven alone, but to be taking others along with him. What a great mercy it is that the Lord is pleased to use the gospel, in spite of our coldness and inadequacy in proclaiming it, to get a hold of the hearts of sinners, and to draw them to the Saviour! That's the work of the Holy Spirit. And that's a work which he does, accompanying the Word.

And the message is the message of reconciliation. There *is* reconciliation in Christ for sinners. It's not reconcilability, but reconciliation. It's not that we have to work out some scheme of reconciliation—the reconciliation is *there* in Christ for sinners, and we have to come and avail ourselves of it—to enter into that relationship of peace through Jesus Christ. That's the call of the gospel, the message of the gospel. It's all been done. There's nothing to do. There's nothing to be done by the sinner. The reconciliation is complete in Christ. 'Be ye reconciled' is a call to avail ourselves of what is in Christ for us.

This call is addressed no doubt to believers who have become estranged from God. That can happen. We feel ourselves at times away from God—our sins have separated between us and him. The apostle is saying to such a person, 'Be ye reconciled.' The way to the restoration of the friendship is open in Christ. There's a returning for the backslider. There's a coming to God for the believer whose soul is saying, 'Where is your God now gone?' Just come back to where you started—to Christ.

And there's a word here to the anxious sinner, who is afraid that the quarrel will never be made up between himself and God. It would be a good thing if there was such an anxious sinner among us, who is feeling estranged from God, and even coming to the conclusion that that's how it's going to end—that's it's never going to be anything different. Ah well, the apostle is saying, God is saying, 'Be ye reconciled to God.' There's reconciliation, there's peace with God through the blood of Christ, for the anxious sinner who feels deserving of the wrath of God and doesn't know how to get out of that predicament.

And also, there's a word for the sinner who is estranged from God, but either doesn't know it or doesn't care about it. This is not much ado about nothing. These are serious matters that are being brought to our attention: reconciliation wrought through the death of the Son of God in our nature. It's not about nothing. It brings home to us the seriousness of our natural condition. And our condition is very serious indeed, if we have no concern about the fact that God and ourselves are enemies, that we are against God and that God is against us. This message of reconciliation is saying to the careless sinner, 'Think about your relationship to God, and realise the danger of going on in this state of alienation. "Seek ye the Lord while he may be found, call ye upon him while he is near: let the wicked forsake his way, and the unrighteous man his thoughts: and let him return unto the Lord, and he will have mercy upon him; and to our God, for he will abundantly pardon.'"

May he bless his Word.

11
Warrants to believe
God's commandment

1 JOHN 3:23
And this is his commandment, That we should believe on the name of his Son Jesus Christ, and love one another, as he gave us commandment.

LORD'S DAY EVENING, 7TH DECEMBER 2008

John tells us that one reason for writing this Epistle was that the readers could come to have the same fellowship with God in Christ which was enjoyed by those who had heard Christ and seen Christ and even touched Christ when he was here on earth. That's one of the great wonders that the Holy Spirit brings about through the Scriptures—that we can have the same communion with God in Christ as the original disciples had, because the physical presence was not what was essential to that communion. We do not know Christ now after the flesh. Perhaps that's what the Lord was teaching Mary when she was about to touch him after his resurrection: 'Touch me not; for I am not yet ascended to my Father' (John 20:17). The old way of communion is in the past, the communion now is to be altogether spiritual. And through the records that we have in the Scriptures, and through the teachings of the apostles, we can come to know Christ as they knew him, and we can come to have fellowship with God in Christ as they had fellowship with him.

And another reason that he gives for writing this Epistle is, 'that your joy may be full'. It was so that the joy that Christians have in God could be as complete as possible—so that we would not be living, as one has said, 'at this poor, dying rate', but that we would be able to grow in grace, to grow in knowledge, to grow in our joy in God through our Lord Jesus Christ.

Another reason that he gives is, that they might know that they have eternal life (1 John 5:13). It was to give assurance of salvation to believers. In the immediate context of these words, the apostle has been dealing with the problems that people have with the assurance of their salvation. Their own heart is condemning them, and they are not able to draw near to God, they're not able to enjoy the sense of belonging to God and having access to God in prayer. He's telling us the conditions in which assurance may be sought and possessed by believers. He's laying emphasis on obedience to the commandments of God, obedience to the revealed will of God. It's not that obedience is the *ground* of fellowship with God, it's not just that it's the *evidence* of fellowship with God, it's not just that it is the *condition* on which fellowship with God is enjoyed—obedience is itself a *part of* that fellowship. It is the believer's response to the love of God which is in Christ Jesus. You see, we can have very airy-fairy ideas of what fellowship with God is. But according to the Word of God, the love of God is flowing to us, and the response of that is, 'We love him, who first loved us' (1 John 4:19). And, 'If ye love me, keep my commandments' (John 14:15). And the obedience of a believing heart is part of that fellowship with God which believers are encouraged to seek and to enjoy. It also is the condition in which assurance of salvation is enjoyed. We cannot enjoy assurance if we are walking contrary to the commandments of the Lord. And here the inspired apostle focuses on this particular commandment, 'that we should believe on the name of his Son Jesus Christ, and love one another, as he gave us commandment.' And that's what I would desire to consider for a little time as enabled this evening—the commandment particularly to believe on the name of his Son Jesus Christ.

As you will recall, in *The Practical Use of Saving Knowledge* we have these 'warrants for believing'—encouragements for sinners to believe in Christ. We have noticed the first one, *God's hearty invitation* addressed to sinners to come to Christ. 'Ho, every one that thirsteth, come ye to the waters.' And then we considered the second one, *his earnest request* that we should be reconciled to him through Christ. That's why he has sent his ambassadors, beseeching us in his name to be reconciled to him. Now, the third warrant is what is called *his strait and awful command* to believe in the Lord Jesus Christ. The idea of the word 'strait' is something that is tightly binding. And 'awful' is 'awe-inspiring.' And when they speak about God's strait and awful command to believe on Jesus Christ, they are speaking about this tightly binding commandment and this awesome, awe-inspiring commandment, to believe on the name of his Son Jesus Christ. That's the commandment—not just a hearty invitation, not just an earnest entreaty, but a very strong, solemn commandment to believe on the name of his Son Jesus Christ.

    1. The object of faith
    2. The nature of faith
    3. The authority for faith
    4. The effect of faith.

1. The object of faith

The object of faith, the one in whom we are to believe, is God's Son—'the name of his Son Jesus Christ'. Of course, the 'name' means everything about him that has been revealed—his person and his work.

The necessity of faith is something that's emphasised throughout the Bible. When the Lord was asked, 'What shall we do, that we might work the works of God?' he said, 'This is the work of God, that ye believe on him whom he hath sent' (John 6:28-29). When a sinner asked, 'What must I do to be saved?' the answer given was, 'Believe on the Lord Jesus Christ, and thou shalt be saved' (Acts 16:30-31). The apostle tells us, 'Without faith it is impossible to please him: for he that cometh to God must believe that he is, and that he is a rewarder of them that diligently seek him' (Hebrews 11:6). 'By grace are ye saved through faith; and that not of yourselves: it is the gift of God' (Ephesians 2:8). We don't need to go over what we're all very well acquainted with—the necessity, if sinners are going to be saved, that they should believe on the Lord Jesus Christ—that they should receive him and rest on him alone for their salvation. The person who doesn't believe on the Lord Jesus Christ cannot be saved. The person who does believe on the Lord Jesus Christ *will* be saved. That's how pivotal, how essential, faith in Jesus Christ is.

Now, Jesus Christ is the object of faith. You hear people talk about having faith in God, and people might say in times of trouble, 'We must have faith in God.' Faith does terminate on God. But it is God as he is revealed in Christ. As he said himself, 'I am the way, the truth, and the life: no man cometh unto the Father, but by me' (John 14:6). We cannot have faith in an absolute God—a God out of Christ—but we have faith in God as he has revealed himself in Jesus Christ. That's what's emphasised again and again. Even Christ himself said concerning the Father, that he desires that the Son would be glorified, that the Son would be honoured. It's both God's way of coming to us, and our way of coming to God—through the Lord Jesus Christ. No one has seen God at any time. No one can stand before an absolute God and expect to be accepted. But God has revealed himself in the Lord Jesus Christ. And that's where faith has to be focused.

'That we should believe on the name of his Son Jesus Christ.' God in our nature: his Son. That's a view of Christ which the apostle John delighted in. He emphasises at the beginning of his Gospel the divine nature of the Lord Jesus. 'In the beginning was the Word, and the Word was with God, and the Word was God' (John 1:1). And the reason that he wrote the Gospel was 'that ye might believe that Jesus is the Christ, the Son of God' (John 20:31). I was quite surprised, looking through this Epistle for references to the Son of God, to see just how numerous they are. And you might find it a profitable exercise to go through the Epistle and see what John has to say and how often he has to speak about the Son of God. This apostle was very much impressed with the divinity of the Saviour, and he's very much emphasising that. Of course, when the Bible speaks about 'the Son of God', it's speaking about someone who is equal with God—who *is* God, in every sense—who possesses all the divine attributes and all the divine powers and all the divine honours. They all belong to this person, who is the object of faith. When we rest in him, we are resting on God, on a divine person.

And the wonder of it is that the name 'his Son' is borne by a person who also has the name Jesus. 'Thou shalt call his name Jesus,' referring to a baby that was to be born (Matthew 1:21). That's a wonder we should never be able to get over, that the name Immanuel—'God with us'—the name of the Son of God, belongs to one who was conceived in the womb of the virgin Mary, and born of her, and who has our nature, who has a human body and a human soul, and who took that human nature so that he could be the Saviour. That's a wonder too—that the name of Saviour should belong to the one whose name is God. A just God, and a Saviour. We've lost—at least, we have to speak for ourselves—we've lost to a large extent the sense of wonder that God against whom we have sinned should be a Saviour, and that in order to be a Saviour, he should take on human nature, so that in that nature he could give obedience in the place of his people and die in the place of his people.

And he did all this as the Lord's appointed, anointed Saviour— 'the Christ'—his Son Jesus Christ. The Son of God was sent into the world, as John tells us, by the Father, appointed by the God against whom we have sinned, to be the Saviour of his people. And when it speaks about his *name*, the *name* of his Son, it's speaking (as I mentioned) not only about the glorious person that he is, but the glorious work that he came to do. John speaks in his first chapter about the blood of Jesus Christ, his Son. He speaks about him being the advocate with the Father, the propitiation for our sins, the one who came as God sent him, in order to take the place of his people and give the obedience that they couldn't give, and die the death that they deserved to die.

We have to believe in this person, Christ the Son of God, crucified, dead, buried, raised again, ascended to God's right hand— that's the kernel of the gospel. That's what Paul was saying when he was writing to the Corinthians, and summing up the gospel that he preached: 'Moreover, brethren, I declare unto you the gospel which I preached unto you, which also ye have received, and wherein ye stand; by which also ye are saved, if ye keep in memory what I preached unto you, unless ye have believed in vain. For I delivered unto you first of all that which I also received, how that Christ died for our sins according to the scriptures, and that he was buried, and that he rose again the third day according to the scriptures' (1 Corinthians 15:1-4). That's the name of our Lord Jesus Christ, God's Son. God in our nature, working out salvation for sinners—doing everything that had to be done to reconcile them to God.

2. The nature of faith

Now, what is the nature of faith in Jesus Christ? What does it mean, that we should believe on the name of his Son Jesus Christ?

Certainly it must mean that we have some acquaintance with the truth concerning him—as we might say, some intellectual acquaintance. Our mind must have some clear view of the truth concerning Jesus Christ. Perhaps that is sometimes where people who are concerned about their soul's salvation go wrong—they don't have a clear view of the truth as it is in Jesus, of the way of salvation as it is in Christ. Martin Luther was like that. When he was reading about the righteousness of God in Romans, he was thinking of the righteousness of God's character, and the righteousness which God requires. He was not realising that what it was speaking about was the righteousness which God has provided. The very thing that was such a fearsome thing to him, such a barrier to him, was the thing that opens the door of hope to sinners—the righteousness of God *in him*.

So we have to have some understanding of the doctrine concerning the Lord Jesus Christ. We're not for a moment suggesting that everyone—that any one—will have a complete understanding or an understanding free from any defect. And the understanding may be very limited. We've read of and known of those whose understandings were very limited. But the Lord revealed to them something concerning the person of Christ and the work of Christ that faith could lay hold of. Faith can't exist in a vacuum. Faith needs to know the truth. If we are seeking the Lord, we should be seeking to have an understanding of the truth of the gospel, the truth concerning the person of Christ and the work of Christ and the way of salvation through the Lord Jesus Christ.

But of course there's more than that. Not only has the mind to be enlightened in these matters, but there must be an acquiescence in that truth, an assent to the truth, an agreement with it, a readiness to believe what has been revealed. We're not going to go to a person in whose existence we don't believe, whatever we read about him. We may have a clear enough acquaintance with the truth concerning Christ, but that truth has to become truth to us. It's truth whether we believe it or not. But before we will act on it, it has to become truth to us—we have to believe what is revealed, we have to acquiesce in it, we have to agree to this way of salvation, we have to agree to the terms of the everlasting gospel. That's a problem some people have. It's a problem we all have by nature, to accept the terms of the gospel. Yes, we may be clear enough about what these terms are, but we have to accept them. Faith can only exist where there is a readiness to accept that Jesus is what he claims to be, and to believe that that is the only way of salvation for a sinner.

And of course, further than that, there has to be this personal entrusting of ourselves to the Saviour—that he will be to us the Saviour that he is to his people. And that's the core of the matter—trusting in the Saviour who has been made known to us in the Word of God and whom we have come to accept is what he claims to be. To be making use of him as our advocate with the Father. To be making use of him as the propitiation for our sins, the one who turns the wrath of God away from those who deserve that wrath, by bearing that wrath himself in their place. To trust in him that what he says will come to pass when he promises, for example, to give rest to those who come to him. The work of faith is described by various terms in the Bible—eating, drinking, tasting, leaning, coming, looking, and so on. But they are all just different illustrations, different expressions, of what it means to trust in the Lord Jesus to be a Saviour to us.

That's the essence of faith. It's not (in the first instance) believing that I am saved. I think sometimes people go through a great deal of torment over this. They think they don't have faith, because they're not able to say, 'I believe that I am saved.' But that's not believing in Jesus. That's not the essence of trust. That's believing in one's own experience, it's having assurance concerning one's own experience. But believing in Christ is hanging on to him for salvation, believing that he is what he claims to be, and casting ourselves on his mercy, whatever thoughts we have about ourselves, whatever assurance we have or do not have. Assurance will come, one way or another, one time or another. It's there, as it were, in the seed of faith—but people may have long to wait for it, as the Confession of Faith says. And it may be intermittent in the experience of some people who are truly the Lord's people. But we have to remember this, that faith is clinging to Christ, cleaving to Christ, casting ourselves on the mercy of God in Jesus Christ, feeling that we are lost, ruined sinners, and we have no hope except in Christ, and being willing to depend upon him for salvation. That's the essence of faith.

You may have questions—'Did I ever believe in Christ? Am I believing in Christ?' But what the soul has to be occupied with is Christ himself, and to be casting oneself on him, whatever will be the outcome. You remember the leper who came to Jesus—he fell on his face before him, and he besought him, saying, 'Lord, if thou wilt, thou canst make me clean' (Luke 5:12). 'Lord, if thou wilt, thou canst make me clean.' There was faith in that! There was an 'if'. There was a question. There was a fear, perhaps: 'Will the Lord do it?' But there was faith in it too—he's able to do it, and I'm asking him to do it for me. Sometimes that may be as far as faith goes. But it's far enough to save the soul. 'I will,' he said, 'be thou clean.' As Lachlan Mackenzie said, 'The beggar had a little note, / 'Lord if thou wilt thou can.' / The banker cashed the little note, / and healed the sickly man.' That's the way it is. Faith has different degrees of strength, and it has different degrees of assurance attaching to it. But basically it's the resting of the soul on the Saviour. The comfort may be more or less—it may be full, it may be absent—but the soul cannot go anywhere else but to Christ. 'Lord, if thou wilt, thou canst make me clean.' There's a cry in that soul, 'Do thou with hyssop sprinkle me, /

I shall be cleansed so' (Psalm 51:7). There's a yearning in that soul for cleansing.

We should believe on the name of his Son Jesus Christ. We should accept the truth concerning him, and we should go to him, to get from him what he's able to give. He's able to save to the uttermost all those who come to God through him (Hebrews 7:25).

3. The authority for faith

Then we have to notice the authority that we have for believing. 'This is his commandment, that we should believe on the name of his Son Jesus Christ.'

We have a hearty invitation. We have an earnest request. But we also have this solemn, serious commandment to believe on the name of his Son Jesus Christ. It's not a case of 'take it or leave it.' It's not a case of 'We can do what we wish to do.' We are under the authority of a commandment from God. Everyone who has ever heard the gospel is confronted with this command. It's as much a command as any of the ten commandments are. It's as much a command as any command that God ever uttered.

I must confess that when I looked at *The Practical Use of Saving Knowledge* and noticed the texts that they were using to support this 'warrant', I wondered about it, because it looks on the surface as if this verse is a commandment to believers to keep on believing. But when you look a little closer, the believing that is referred to in this verse is not the ongoing believing of the believer, but it's the initial decisive act of faith. The grammatical form makes that very clear. What is being spoken of in this verse is not the ongoing attitude of faith (although of course there will be an ongoing attitude of faith), but the first step in the life of the Christian. The commandment is, 'Believe on the name of his Son Jesus Christ, and love one another, as he gave us commandment' (1 John 3:23).

The command is to believe. And the command comes to sinners in all sorts of conditions, in all sorts of attitudes. I've brought in a little note from *The Practical Use*, where they're talking about this commandment, and this is what they say. 'Every one who heareth the gospel must make conscience of the duty of lively faith in Christ. The weak believer must not think it presumption to do what is commanded. The person inclined to desperation must take up himself and think upon obedience unto this sweet and saving command. The strong believer must dip yet more in the sense of his need he hath of Jesus Christ, and more and more grow in the obedience of this command. Yea, the most impenitent, profane and wicked person must not thrust out himself or be thrust out by others from orderly aiming at this duty, how desperate so ever his condition seems to be. For he that commands all men to believe on Christ doth thereby command all men to believe that they are damned and lost without Christ. He therefore commands all men to acknowledge their sins, and their need of Christ, and in effect commands all men to repent that they may believe on him. And whosoever do refuse to repent of their bygone sins are guilty of disobedience to this command, given to all hearers, but especially to those that are within the visible church. For this is his commandment, that we should believe on the name of his Son Jesus Christ.'

The command is a command to all, everywhere, who hear the gospel of the grace of God. God now commandeth all men everywhere to repent. He commands sinners to believe on the name of his Son Jesus Christ.

And you find that throughout the Scriptures. You find that what is going to condemn sinners at last, as we have it in Thessalonians, is that they did not obey the gospel (2 Thessalonians 1:8). Those who hear the gospel have many sins. They have many things in their lives to condemn them. But there's nothing that can condemn them, or that will condemn them, if they believe on the name of his Son Jesus Christ. But not believing on the name of Son Jesus Christ leaves them exposed to condemnation—not only for all the sins that remain unforgiven, but especially for this greatest sin of all, which is doing despite to the Son of God, treating him with contempt. God is displeased with those who will not trust in the Lord Jesus Christ. Just think of the affront that is done to God, the affront that is done to

Christ, when a sinner says, either in as many words or by his actions, that he cannot believe, he will not believe, in the Lord Jesus Christ.

Now of course there is a sinful inability to obey the commandment in every one of us. No sinner has the power to believe in the Lord Jesus Christ. That is something which sinners are often confronted with when they try, as it were, to believe in the Lord Jesus Christ. They feel so unable, so helpless, in the face of the commandment. But of course, the inability to keep the commandment is not an excuse, because the inability arises from the sinfulness of the human heart—the same sinfulness that renders a person unable to keep the law of God. 'The carnal mind is enmity against God: for it is not subject to the law of God, neither indeed can be' (Romans 8:7). And neither can the carnal mind be subject to this commandment to believe on the name of his Son Jesus Christ. That's just a demonstration of how lost we are by nature. Here we are, lost and ruined by our sin, and we're confronted by the sad outcome of that, that there's nothing awaiting us but the wrath of God—and here comes the joyful sound: there's salvation in Christ! All you have to do is believe in the Lord Jesus Christ and you'll be saved! And there is the sinner, and perhaps he feels he's hanging by a thread over the mouth of hell—and there's deliverance, there's a Saviour who's able to save to the uttermost all who come to God through him. And that sinner is struck with this: 'I cannot believe in him! It's my only hope, and yet I cannot do it! I'm lost, ruined, helpless, on account of sin.'

And still the command comes, that we should believe on the name of his Son Jesus Christ. And that inability, that helplessness, is not only not an excuse because of the fact that it's accounted for by our sin. It's also not an excuse, because faith comes from the grace of God. We can't bring faith to God. We have to get it from God. 'By grace are ye saved through faith; and that not of yourselves: it is the gift of God' (Ephesians 2:8). It's there, for sinners, in the grace of God. What we need is to be brought completely to an end of ourselves, so that we will cast ourselves on the mercy of God to give us that grace that we need to believe in the Lord Jesus Christ.

The command is bearing down on us—a gracious command, a sweet command, a precious commandment. And we are so unable. But these two things brought together are just pressing us to this point where there's no hope for us but in the mercy of God in Christ Jesus. And that's what we're not willing to come to terms with, to the extent to which we are left to ourselves. We don't *want* to be debtors to the mercy of God, whatever we say, however we delude ourselves into thinking that it's otherwise. Although we know we can't, we *want* to have something to bring us to God. We want to be able to come to God, whereas we need God to bring us. The commandment is pressing down on us, it's encouraging us, it's showing us where our safety lies, and it's bringing us to the point where we realise how dependent we are on the divine mercy.

Yes, the commandment is there, and the authority of God is behind the invitation and the request and the commandment. The authority of the God of heaven! That's why, when a sinner comes to Christ and trusts in Christ, that sinner can be assured of salvation, assured of a welcome. How did you come in hither? You came because the Lord commanded you to come. And he accompanied the command with his powerful call, the call of the Spirit of God, and you were made willing to come. And with such authority behind your coming, you can be sure you will never be cast out. 'All that the Father giveth me shall come to me; and him that cometh to me I will in no wise cast out' (John 6:37).

The authority is in the commandment, and when we have arguments against our coming, we have to face up to the fact that God has commanded us to come. It's not that we don't have authority for coming. We're not *willing* to come. And we're not willing to come, because of our sinful nature, because we're not as convinced as we should be about our lostness, because we're too much tied to our own righteousness, we're too much tied to the things of time and sense. We need all these cords to be broken, so that we can respond gladly to this commandment of the Lord. If there's a soul—a poor, lost, ruined sinner—who is desiring to come to Christ, desiring to be saved by Christ, then there's nothing outside of yourself to keep you from him. Everything on his side—the invitation, the request, the commandment—is encouraging the sinner to come to the Saviour. All the obstacles, all the objections, arise from what is within ourselves. 'This is his commandment, that we should believe on the name of his Son Jesus Christ.'

4. The effect of faith

And then, when a person does believe, the effect that is to follow is, 'Love one another, as he gave us commandment.'

The Lord Jesus commanded his disciples—you have it in John's Gospel—that they were to love one another. And John is emphasising that very much in this Epistle. If God has loved us, if God has shed abroad his love in our hearts, if we love God in response to that love, then we will love one another. We will love all the brethren.

There are different kinds of love. There's a love for God, there's a love for the brethren, and there's a love for our fellow human beings in general. The Lord's people must feel a compassion in their souls for sinners that are on the broad way that leads to destruction. It's very solemn to see the crowds, young and old, going through the streets of the city, all busy in one way or another or seeking pleasure, and all on the way to eternity. And where are they going to be in eternity? When we see these sinners, so oblivious to the reality of eternal things, you would like to just be able to take hold of them and lead them into some sense of reality.

But there's a special love mentioned here for the brethren—for those who are the Lord's people, who share our faith in Jesus Christ. How can we say that we love God, whom we have not seen, if we don't love those whom we have seen, who are his children? (1 John 4:20). You might say, 'Well, it's much easier to love God than it is to love some of his children.' But the Word of God stands, that if we do love God, then we will love his children, our brethren. And we'll love them in a practical way. As the apostle is saying in this chapter, in verses 18 and 19, 'My little children, let us not love in word, neither in tongue; but in deed and in truth. And hereby we know that we are of the truth, and shall assure our hearts before him.'

This is one of the things that gives an evidence of faith, that helps to give assurance that we belong to the family of God—when we love those who belong to that family. And I think the Lord's people, when they're pressed, they can say that—even the unassured Christian, the Christian who's wondering whether he or she is a Christian at all. Who are your people? Altogether apart from happiness and woe, who would you like to spend eternity with? The godless, wicked, Christless souls? Or those who love the Lord, and who have been saved by his grace? You feel like Ruth, 'Thy people shall be my people, and thy God my God' (Ruth 1:16). And like the psalmist, 'I am a companion of all them that fear thee' (Psalm 119:63). Someone suggested that when the psalmist said 'I am a companion of all them that fear thee,' he might have been thinking, 'Well, I can't say that I fear thee myself, but these are the people that I long to be with.' I'm not sure that that's the right interpretation, but sometimes that is the case with the Lord's people. 'Whatever I have to say about myself,' the Christian may be saying, 'and I have my doubts, I have my questions, I have my anxieties as to whether or not I belong to these people. But these are my people, these are my companions, these are the people that I like to be with, and that I hope to be with, and I would wish to be with throughout eternity— those who love God and keep his commandments, those who trust in the Lord Jesus Christ, those who have the fruit of the Spirit, however limited that may be.'

'Love the brethren!' That's the fruit of faith. We can't love the brethren without faith, and we can't believe without coming to love the brethren. These things go together. Faith is the first step that the little newborn child of God takes in the Christian life, and it's a life that's characterised by love—love to God, and love to his people, and love to the souls of men.

It's in this context, the apostle says, that you're going to get assurance of your salvation—if you have regard to this commandment, 'Believe on the name of his Son Jesus Christ, and love the brethren, as he gave us commandment.' That's what we ought to be concerned about as sinners, and as people who may be trusting in the Lord and yet have questions about it. We have to concentrate on the commandment—what the Lord is requiring of us. Faith in Christ, followed by love for the brethren.

That's the third of these warrants for believing on Jesus Christ. Yes, God gives us a hearty invitation, 'Come to the waters,' and he makes an earnest request, 'Be ye reconciled to God!' But he also gives us this very strict and awe-inspiring commandment. 'Believe on the name of his Son Jesus Christ, and love one another!'

You remember there was a man who came to Jesus with an arm that was withered. He had no strength in it at all. The Lord said, 'Stretch forth your hand, stretch forth your arm!' And he stretched it forth. Well, you can try to analyse the psychology of that, but that's the way it has always been. The command has come to people who couldn't obey the command, and they obeyed the command—because the command was accompanied with power.

We have to seek grace to obey the commandment of God. There are no excuses for not obeying. There is grace in God, and we need to realise our need of that grace. But what we have to do with is the commandment of the Lord. God has said, 'Believe!' And no reason, no excuse will stand in the face of unbelief. When he is come—the Spirit of truth—he will reprove the world of sin, because they believe not on me (John 16:8-9).

May the Lord bless his Word to us.

12

Warrants to believe
The assurance of life

JOHN 3:35-36

The Father loveth the Son, and hath given all things into his hand. He that believeth on the Son hath everlasting life: and he that believeth not the Son shall not see life; but the wrath of God abideth on him.

LORD'S DAY EVENING, 14TH DECEMBER 2008

We have been trying to consider some of the warrants that are given to sinners to believe in the Lord Jesus Christ. Following the pattern of *The Practical Use of Saving Knowledge*, we began by thinking about the *hearty invitation* which God gives to sinners, for example when he says in Isaiah 55, 'Ho, every one that thirsteth, come ye to the waters.' Then we thought about what's called the *earnest request* that God makes to sinners to be reconciled to him through Christ, as we have it in 2 Corinthians 5, 'Be ye reconciled to God.' Then last Sabbath we were thinking of the *strait and awful command* of God, that command which ties us in, that command which has all the awesome authority of God behind it, as we have it in John's First Epistle, 'This is his commandment, that ye should believe on the name of his Son Jesus Christ, and love one another.'

Now we come to the fourth and last of these warrants for sinners to believe in Christ, where the Scriptures are assuring us that life belongs to those who believe in the Son of God, and assuring us that condemnation remains on those who do not. The assurance of life to believers, and the assurance of condemnation to unbelievers, is surely pressing upon us the urgency and the necessity, and the warrant that we have, for believing on the Son of God.

1. As the Lord may enable me, I'd like to begin by saying something about the person on whom we are to believe. 'The Father loveth the Son, and hath given all things into his hand.'

2. Then in the second place, we might consider what it is that distinguishes one sinner from another. That is, of course, their relationship to Christ—whether they believe in Christ or not. That's the one fundamental distinction that runs through the whole human race.

3. Then the third thing we might consider is the life that belongs to believers.

4. And finally, the condemnation that rests on unbelievers.

1. The one on whom we are to believe

Well, the one in whom we are to believe is set before us here as God's Son. The Father loves him, and the Father has given all things into his hand.

There has been some discussion about who actually spoke these words. Certainly John the Baptist was the speaker to his disciples in the earlier part, when he said, 'A man can receive nothing' (verse 27). There's no reason to think that he is not the speaker throughout the remainder of the chapter. The other alternative would be that it is John the apostle himself who is expanding on what John the Baptist said, but there's no reason to think that. There's a unity throughout the whole speech, addressed by John the Baptist to his disciples, and there is nothing in it which was not in keeping with what John the Baptist had already been declaring. We find that he has been speaking of Jesus as the Christ, as the one whose shoe's latchet he was not worthy to unloose. He was speaking about him as the Son of God. He was speaking about him as the Lamb of God, which taketh away the sin of the world. He had the truth about Christ revealed to him by the Holy Spirit. 'I wouldn't have known any of this at all,' he said himself, 'but that it was revealed to me by the Holy Spirit.'

In the previous verses, he has been saying some wonderful things about Christ. Perhaps we don't always appreciate just how full and rich was the testimony that John the Baptist gave to Christ. He speaks about him as the Christ, before whom he was sent. He speaks about him having received what he got from heaven. He speaks about him as the bridegroom of the Church, the one who's going to increase, and before whom John and everyone else will decrease. He speaks about him as the one who is sent by God and who speaks the words of God and who possesses the Spirit of God without any measure. A very high testimony to Jesus Christ!

But notice just for a little this particular testimony: 'The Father loveth the Son, and hath given all things into his hand.' He's speaking about Jesus as the Son—the Son of the Father, the Son of God. That's really a wonderful thing, when you realise that Jesus and John were blood relatives. Their mothers were cousins. This is someone whose humanity John was perfectly assured of. And yet, by the teaching of the Holy Spirit, John is equally sure that this person is the Son of God, that he possesses a divine character: divine powers belong to him.

He's the only begotten Son, as the other John says, in the bosom of the Father (John 1:18). He's the one who created all things. He's the one who is the light and life of the world. He is God in every sense of the word. That's the main implication of the name 'the Son of God'. Whatever it tells us about the mysterious eternal relationship between the Father and the Son, it is not teaching us any inferiority, because the Son is equal with the Father in every respect. The Son is just as eternal as the Father, just as infinite as the Father, just as unchangeable as the Father is. This is the person who has come in God's name to save sinners—not a mere man. Yes, a real man—true humanity belongs to Christ, the same humanity we have ourselves, although free from sin. But he is much more than a man. He's the man who is God's fellow. He is the Son of God with power. All the honour that belongs to God belongs to him. That's what makes him such a suitable Saviour for sinners. That's how he can bear the burden of his people's sin, the burden of their salvation—because he's not a mere man, but his humanity is the humanity of God the

Son. That is the great mystery of godliness, God manifest in the flesh (1 Timothy 3:16).

And what John is saying is, 'The Father loveth the Son.' The Son is the object of the Father's love. Of course, that is true with regard to the eternal relationship between the eternal Father and the eternal Son. It was a relationship—it *is* a relationship, an ever-present relationship—of love. God is love. Within the Godhead is the most infinite, eternal, unchangeable manifestation of love. That is a distinctive of Christianity—the God of the Christian, the only God there really is, is a living being, within whom there is a fellowship of love. You don't hear much of the love of Allah, who doesn't exist anyway. But God is love, and supposing there was no creature outside of God, God is love, and there is infinite, eternal scope for the love which God is, to be exercised. The Father loves the Son, and the Son loves the Father. There's this eternal mutual love and satisfaction.

But what we have to notice is that that love embraces the Son, not just in his eternal being as the Son of God, but also when he takes on himself the humanity of his people—when he enters into the office of their Redeemer, when he becomes the Christ of God, as it were. The Father loves the Son as the head of the body which is the Church. He loves the Son in connection with his people, embracing his people, embodying his people. We see this at the baptism of Jesus. When Jesus was baptised, the Spirit descended upon him, and a voice from heaven was heard—by some at least—to say, 'This is my beloved Son.' *This* is my beloved Son—the one who was baptised into union with sinners who needed repentance, the one who has come in God's great name to save, the one who has taken on himself that nature which is a little lower than the angels. *This* is my beloved Son, the Son of my love, in whom I am well pleased. 'The Father loveth the Son.' The Son on earth, in our nature, as the Redeemer of his people, is the object of the Father's love. He's embraced in that love, and all of his people are embraced in that love along with him.

What a great encouragement that is, when we think of Christ, and when we think of him not only as the Son in the bosom of the Father, but as the Son in our nature, and we realise that the eternal love of God embraces him in that nature, and embraces him in that connection with his people. The Father is approving of the Son as the Son comes to do the work he gave him to do. And the Father is surrounding him with his love, and surrounding those who are united to him, with his love.

'And he hath given all things into his hand.' Of course, as the Son of God, everything belonged to him, everything belongs to him. The fulness of the Godhead is his. It wasn't given to him—it belongs to him, the only begotten, the eternal Son of God. But John is speaking about the Son in his capacity as the Christ, as the Redeemer of his people. The Son in our nature, the Son as our Saviour—the Father has given all things into his hand. He gave him his people to save. He gave him the power to save them. He gave him the qualifications. He gave him the Spirit without measure. He laid up the whole of our salvation in Christ Jesus. 'All power in heaven and in earth is given unto me'—power to save his people.

He is the judge, he is the sustainer, he is the Saviour of his people. All things are in his hand. The working out of salvation, and the glory that was going to come to him through the working out of that salvation—the Father has given it to him. The Father sent the Son to be the Saviour of the world. 'God so loved the world, that he gave his only begotten Son' (John 3:16), and he gave his Son all that he needed—all the power he needed, all the authority he needed, the Spirit without measure—so that he could accomplish that work. The Father has entrusted everything to his Son.

'All things are delivered unto me of my Father.' No one knows the Son but the Father, and no one knows the Father but the Son, and he to whomsoever the Son will reveal him (Matthew 11:27). Everything is in Christ's hand. He is the Mediator between God and men. If we need anything in relation to God, we have to go to Christ for it. You remember how, when Paul was writing to the Corinthians, he said, 'God has made him to be unto us wisdom, and righteousness, and sanctification, and redemption' (1 Corinthians 1:30). He said to the Ephesians that they obtained 'all spiritual blessings in heavenly places in Christ Jesus' (Ephesians 1:3). Everything has been laid up in Christ—the fulness of blessing. 'It pleased the Father that in him should all fulness dwell' (Colossians 1:19). 'And of his fulness have all we received, and grace for grace' (John 1:16).

The souls of his people—the salvation of his people—is in the hands of the Saviour. You remember the poor man, regarded as a simple man, who was asked, 'Do you have a soul?' And he said, 'No, I don't have a soul.' I suppose they were shaking their heads at his ignorance. But he explained what he meant, and the gist of it was, 'I had a soul once, but it was lost, and Jesus found it, and I have left it in his keeping, and therefore I don't have a soul.' Now, whatever one might say about the theology or the logic of it, he was getting at the very root of the matter—everything is in Christ's hands. In our own hands, everything would be lost, but everything connected with our salvation is in the hands of Christ. 'The Father hath given all things into his hands.'

This is the person in whom we are to believe—the Son of God, the eternal Son of God in our nature, embraced in the love of God the Father. That's where sinners get to know the love of God. The love of God is not a general thing—it's something that is in Christ, and it is those who are in Christ who are embraced in that love. And everything is in his hands. All he needs to save his people, all the rich resources of grace and glory, are Christ's to give. The fulness that is in him is not just for himself—it's for distributing to his people. He is the fountain. It's not a cistern, shut up, but a fountain, from which the streams of grace and mercy flow to sinners.

2. What distinguishes one sinner from another

The second thing to notice is what it is that distinguishes one sinner from another, and that is their relation to Christ—whether or not they believe on him. 'He that believeth on the Son hath everlasting life, and he that believeth not the Son shall not see life, but the wrath of God abideth on him.'

You remember Paul said to the Romans, 'There is no difference.' There's no difference. 'For *all* have sinned, and come short of the glory of God' (Romans 3:22-23). You have the difference between the Pharisee and the publican, you have the difference between the respectable person and the profligate person, the difference between the Jew and the Gentile—there are lots of differences one might see if they just look at the externals. But the Bible says, 'There's no difference, for all have sinned.' The whole human race is in the same boat as far as this is concerned—'*all* have sinned and come short of the glory of God.' What distinguishes one from another is whether or not they believe on the Son of God. This is a dividing line that runs through the whole human race.

It's interesting and instructive to just remark that within this one verse there are two different Greek words used for 'believing'. The first word, 'he that believeth on the Son,' is the usual straightforward word for believing or trusting or being persuaded. But the second one, 'he that believeth not,' is translated elsewhere as 'not being willing to be persuaded'—not yielding, not obeying. Unbelief and disobedience are equated with each other so that the terms are interchangeable. Believing is obeying the command of the gospel, and unbelief is disobeying the command of the gospel. The gospel has been sent into all nations, Paul said to the Romans, for the obedience of faith. When he was writing to the Thessalonians he spoke about the dreadful day of judgment, when Christ will come, and the dreadful consequences that will come upon unbelievers, 'those that obey not the gospel' (2 Thessalonians 1:8). They obey not the gospel. Unbelief is disobedience to the command of God.

Now when you think of believers and unbelievers, on the side of the unbeliever there are many who have never heard the gospel of the grace of God. They have never heard the gospel. That means that they continue to be in the state in which they were born and brought up. They continue to be the sinners that they were. While their condition is not so aggravated as those who have heard the gospel, their condition is the condition of sinners who are justly exposed to the wrath of God. You remember how the apostle said to the Romans that there are people who have never heard the law, but that those that are without the law shall be judged without the law. 'As many as have sinned without law shall also perish without law: and as many as have sinned in the law shall be judged by the law' (Romans

2:12). Because the Gentiles who didn't have the law were a law to themselves, the law was written on their hearts, their conscience was bearing witness, their thoughts were accusing or else excusing one another (Romans 2:14-15). Supposing they never heard a word of the gospel or a word of the law, they have enough knowledge reflected in their conscience to condemn them for their sins. The sinner who has never heard the gospel is a sinner who is under the displeasure of God, under the curse of God, without any claim on the mercy of God.

But also on the side of the unbeliever there are those who *have* heard the gospel of the grace of God. They continue in the state in which they were born and brought up, because they will not believe the gospel that they hear. Only the gospel can rescue them from the state of sin and misery in which they are by nature, and their unbelief, their lack of belief, has this character of disobedience to a commandment, to an invitation, to a request, which has been clearly made known to them in the everlasting gospel. Therefore, while those who have never heard the gospel will perish in their sins, there is an added element of condemnation in the experience of those who have heard and yet have despised and have rejected and refused to believe the gospel of the grace of God.

But what characterises all the people on the one side of the line is that they have no relationship with Christ. They have no confidence in Christ, they don't trust in him as their Saviour. There's a great variety within that group, but they all have in common that they are still in their sins, and they are still under God's displeasure, and that is because they lack the faith that would take them out of that situation.

And on the other side, there are those who believe in the Son of God. They might be every bit as bad as the others, in themselves, and certainly that's how they appear to themselves. If there's anything true about a person who has experienced the saving grace of God, it's this—that there's not a person in all the human race that they can look down on, as if they were more worthy of the mercy of God than that person. Paul was not just using rhetorical arts when he said, 'I am the chief of sinners' (1 Timothy 1:15). He meant what he said. There wasn't a sinner that he would put ahead of himself in the league of sinners, because he was taken up with what he was himself in relation to God. The believer in the Son of God is a sinner in his own estimation. But what rescues him, what distinguishes him from other sinners, is that he has been brought into a relationship with Christ that is characterised by faith in the Saviour.

So we have to continue and complete what Paul said to the Romans when he said there is no difference. 'There is no difference: for all have sinned, and come short of the glory of God; being justified freely by his grace through the redemption that is in Christ Jesus: whom God hath set forth to be a propitiation through faith in his blood, to declare his righteousness for the remission of sins that are past, through the forbearance of God; to declare, I say, at this time his righteousness: that he might be just, and the justifier of him which believeth in Jesus. Where is boasting then? It is excluded. By what law? of works? Nay: but by the law of faith.' (Romans 3:22-27). Where there is a difference, it's faith that makes the difference—the faith which is the gift of God. 'By grace are ye saved through faith; and that not of yourselves: it is the gift of God' (Ephesians 2:8).

You see, when we're thinking of this distinction, we would have to trace it back ultimately to the sovereign, free grace and mercy of God, who gives faith to sinners. But we're thinking just now on the level of the sinner himself. And what makes the difference between the person who has life and the person who is under the wrath of God? It's that one of them has been brought to believe in the Lord Jesus Christ. It doesn't matter what kind of sinner he was before. The sinner who believes in Jesus is justified from all things, and therefore saved from the wrath which is to come.

That is something we should think about ourselves, as we find ourselves under the gospel of the grace of God. In any congregation, what makes the difference between one person and another is this, that the one is believing on the Son of God, and the other is not believing on the Son of God. We might all look the same outwardly, we might all live the same as far as externals are concerned, we might all be religious, we might all be respectable, we might all genuinely respect the things of God. But probe beneath the surface. What makes the difference between one and the other? The one believes and the other does not. That's why it is such an important question, 'Dost thou believe on the Son of God?' Ultimately, nothing else matters because everything is bound up with that. Dost thou believe on the Son of God?

3. The life that belongs to believers

Now the third thing is the life that belongs to those who believe on the Son of God. 'He that believeth on the Son of God hath everlasting life.'

'I am come,' Christ said, 'that they might have life, and that they might have it more abundantly' (John 10:10). The life that is being spoken of, of course, is much more than existence, and much more than eternal existence. Eternal existence is something that belongs to every rational creature. We will never go out of existence, whatever our spiritual condition is. Sometimes that can come as quite a dread-inspiring thought, if we have any uncertainty as to our relation to God, our relation to Christ. The thought of living for ever, existing for ever, is a terrible thought. One feels a great measure of compassion and sorrow for those who act under the deluded impression that death is the end of their troubles, that death is going to take them into a state of non-existence. It's a fearful thing to hasten the time of our departure from this world, when we realise there's an eternity of existence beyond, for each one of us.

It's not merely eternal existence, but it's eternal existence in the favour and in the fellowship of God. 'This is life eternal, that they might know thee the only true God, and Jesus Christ, whom thou hast sent' (John 17:3)—a life lived in God's favourable presence, a life lived enjoying God. 'In thy presence is fulness of joy; at thy right hand there are pleasures for evermore' (Psalm 16:11). That's the prospect before the Lord's people. It's in the promise. They have everlasting life in prospect, they have everlasting life in the promise of God.

But they also have everlasting life in possession. They've got the beginnings of it in their souls here and now. They've been delivered from the destructive power of natural death, they've been delivered from the power of spiritual death, and they've been delivered from the prospect of eternal death. They are *alive* toward God. 'The life which I now live in the flesh I live by the faith of the Son of God' (Galatians 2:20). He's not talking about his animal [physical] existence, but his spiritual relationship with God.

Of course, everlasting life in the soul here will have effects that it will not have in heaven. The existence of everlasting life in a soul here will cause trouble as well as blessing, because it creates a conflict with the sin that doth so easily beset us. That's something that will not exist in heaven. It's a sign of life, a sign of everlasting life, when sin really troubles a person, and takes them to Christ, to the fountain that is opened for sin and for uncleanness, and makes them plead with the Holy Spirit to renew them and to give them the victory over the sin that troubles them so much.

'He that believeth on the Son of God hath everlasting life.' He's got the life of justification. He's no longer under the sentence of condemnation because of his sin, but he's clothed in the righteousness of Christ, living as a righteous person before God, because the righteousness of Christ is imputed to him. He's got the life of adoption—the life of a son in the Father's house, very different from that of an alien, very different from that of a servant. He's got the life of sanctification—he's got the Holy Spirit in him, giving him desires he wouldn't otherwise have, giving him abilities he wouldn't otherwise have, to believe and to repent and to obey, to will and to do to some extent according to God's good pleasure (Philippians 2:13). He's got the life of grace in the soul now, and the life of glory in the world to come. Grace, as has often been said, is young glory—grace is glory in the bud. 'Now are we the sons of God, and it doth not yet appear what we shall be: but we know that, when he shall appear, we shall be like him; for we shall see him as he is' (1 John 3:2).

'He that believeth on the Son hath everlasting life.' He possesses life that shall never end (Psalm 133:3). As that old minister on his deathbed said when he was asked, 'How are you?' 'Well, I'm alive, alive and no more. But remember,' he said, 'it's alive for evermore.'

That's the way it is with the Lord's people, those who believe on the Lord Jesus Christ. Your life is hid with Christ in God. When Christ, who is our life, shall appear, we shall appear with him in glory (Colossians 3:3-4).

The wonderful thing is that this life belongs to those who believe. They receive Christ and they rest on him alone for salvation, and everlasting life is theirs. It doesn't cost them anything. It's not won by their own endeavours. It cost the Son of God in our nature a great deal—it cost him his death on the cross of Calvary, such a death as we can't begin to imagine. How the Son in the bosom of the Father in our nature could be shut out from the favour of God and the fellowship of God in his own consciousness, so that he says, 'My God, my God, why hast thou forsaken me?' (Psalm 22:1). He died. The death of Christ is much more than a physical experience, the separation of soul and body. In fact, the separation of soul and body is something that took place when he had already plumbed the depths of that death. And after saying, 'My God, my God, why hast thou forsaken me?' he came back to the peacefulness that enabled him to say, 'Father, into thy hands I commend my spirit,' and having said that, he gave up the ghost (Luke 23:46). Physical death was a part of the curse which he endured, but the curse went much deeper and wider than that. And all of this was so that, because he died, we would not die. As someone said, 'He die; me no die.' That's at the heart of the gospel. Some of the most profound of gospel statements have been uttered by people who could hardly put two words together, and that person certainly got to the very root—the very heart—of the gospel: 'He die; me no die.'

He that believeth on the Son hath everlasting life. What a glorious position to be in, a sinner on the earth tonight, wrestling on toward heaven against wind and storm and tide, contending with the world and the flesh and the devil, and yet having the present possession, having the promise, having the future prospect, of everlasting life—living in the presence of God. It must be a wonderful thing, to be found in Christ, and to be found in heaven, and no barrier between oneself and the enjoyment of God.

4. The condemnation which rests on unbelievers

But then, you see, the other side, finally—the condemnation which abides on the unbeliever. 'He that believeth not the Son shall not see life; but the wrath of God abideth on him.'

He that believeth not, if he doesn't have Christ, if he's not resting upon the Son of God for salvation, he 'shall not see life.' He won't see it. He won't taste it. He won't experience it. He'll never know what it is to have life. Yes, he will have existence, but it will not be an existence that can be called life. It will be an eternal death.

It's a pity we can say things like that and hear them and realise so little the awfulness of it. Eternal death—eternal separation from God, and yet never getting away from God. Eternal confrontation with the fact of God and the demands of God and our own sin. Eternal existence, and yet not a spark of life—no spiritual life, no eternal life, no enjoyment of God.

He'll not see life, but 'the wrath of God abideth on him.' The wrath of God was on him, and the wrath of God continues to be on the person who does not believe. The wrath of God is on us all by nature. Paul said, 'We are the children of wrath, even as others' (Ephesians 2:3). That was our natural state. Condemned already. The sentence has gone forth: 'The soul that sins shall die' (Ezekiel 18:4).

There is a way of deliverance in Christ. And here is a person who has not availed himself of that way of deliverance. The wrath of God abideth on him. He's still in that position. Although he has heard the gospel—although the way of salvation has been before his mind, all his days perhaps—he doesn't believe on the Son of God, he's not resting on the Son of God for salvation, and therefore the wrath of God abides on him—the wrath of God for all the sins that remain unforgiven. What's going to blot out the sin—any sin—of any sinner who doesn't come to the fountain that is opened for sin and for uncleanness? What *can* wash away our sins, if we don't come to Christ and to the fountain opened for sin and for uncleanness? All our tears will not wash away our sins. All our resolutions, all our alleged good works, will not blot out our sins. So the wrath of God abides on that sinner, who hasn't come to the fountain of cleansing.

But that sinner, who has heard of the Son whom God has loved and the Son to whom God has given everything, and doesn't believe in him—the wrath of God is on him for his unbelief as well as for his sins that he continues to be guilty of before God. Unbelief is the crowning sin of all. Jesus said, 'When the Spirit is come, he will reprove the world of sin, because they believe not on me' (John 16:8-9). He'll reprove them of all the sin that has been consequently unforgiven—he'll demonstrate it to them, he'll convince them of it, he'll show them it—but he'll also show them that what has kept that sin to their account was their failure to believe in the Lord Jesus Christ. If only they had believed in Christ, their sins would have been blotted out.

Unbelief, in a person who hears the gospel, amounts to trampling the Son of God underfoot, or as the Bible says, despising the blood of the everlasting covenant. It's a very serious matter, not to believe the testimony that God has given concerning his Son. It's the greatest sin that any person could commit, to despise Christ, to neglect the great salvation, to refuse to put our confidence in him, to refuse to believe the testimony God has given concerning him. The wrath of God abideth on such a person.

The wrath of God is a terrible thing, because it's not a sudden springing up of emotion, as it is in human beings. Some people are much quicker than others in their tempers, and they can flare up, and then go down again as quickly. That's not what characterises God. The wrath of God is the determined opposition of God in his holiness to sin, and his determination to punish sin. It's a very sober and solemn deliberation on his part. It arises from his holiness, it arises from the justice of his character, it arises from the hatred which he has for sin. It's not a bubbling up of some emotion. It's an essential characteristic of the nature of God, that he hates sin, and that he will punish the sinner.

It's because the righteous Lord loveth righteousness (Psalm11:7). That's the fountain of it. It's his love for righteousness that makes him angry with the sinner every day. As the apostle wrote to the Hebrews, 'It is a fearful thing to fall into the hands of the living God'

(Hebrews 10:31). And as he said again in that Epistle, 'Our God is a consuming fire' (Hebrews 12:29). That's what he said at the end of a chapter where he had been celebrating the grace and mercy of God. It's not a contradiction of grace, it's not a contradiction of mercy. The grace of God and the mercy of God are the grace and mercy of one who is glorious in holiness, and that holiness manifests itself in a hatred of sin and in wrath against the sinner.

That wrath is just as eternal as the life of the believer is. Everlasting means everlasting, whether it's applied to the blessedness of the redeemed in heaven, or the sad condition of the lost in hell. There's no end to it. No end to heaven, and no end to hell.

These things are brought to our attention by the Spirit in the Word in order to press on us the necessity for believing in the Son of God. As we saw in the morning in connection with the covenant of works in Genesis 2, on the one hand, there is this solemn threat, 'in the day thou eatest thereof, thou shalt surely die,' and on the other hand, there is the tree of life in the midst of the garden, promising life to the one who would continue with God. So it is here. There is life and death. There's grace and there is justice. There's eternal blessedness, and there's eternal woe. And what makes the difference is our relationship with the Lord Jesus Christ. Dost thou believe on the Son of God?

When you go back over the chapter we've read, you see how necessary faith is. God so loved the world, that he gave his only begotten Son, that whosoever believeth in him should not perish, but have everlasting life. And when you go further back, you find how necessary it is that we should be born again if we are to have faith. Except a man be born of water and of the Spirit, he's not going to see the kingdom of God, he's not going to enter into it. This is what is being pressed upon us. You must believe. 'What must I do to be saved?' 'Believe in the Lord Jesus Christ, and thou shalt be saved.' 'But oh, how can I believe in him? This is my solemn responsibility under God.' Whether you're Nicodemus or whether you're the thief on the cross, you must be born again. It's not an easy thing, it's not a natural thing, it's not something within the capacity of the sinner to believe. But sinners *do* believe, and the reason they believe is because they are born again of the Spirit of God. Heaven and hell are set before us here. We are being urged to realise the necessity of being born again and being brought to a living faith in Christ.

May he bless his Word.

13

Faith without works is dead

JAMES 2:19-20
Thou believest that there is one God; thou doest well: the devils also believe, and tremble. But wilt thou know, O vain man, that faith without works is dead?

LORD'S DAY MORNING, 14TH AUGUST 2011

These solemn words appear in the course of the argument that the apostle is presenting in support of his statement that faith without works is dead. We have to realise that James, in writing his Epistle, has a very different object in view than Paul had in writing his Epistles. Some people try to suggest that there is a conflict or a contradiction between the teaching of the apostle Paul, that a sinner is justified by faith without works, and the teaching of James, that a sinner is not justified by a faith which is not accompanied by works. But the apostles are counteracting different dangerous heresies.

The apostle Paul is counteracting the legalism that is in the human soul and that comes to expression in so many different ways. It was coming to expression in the suggestion that faith in Christ was not enough—that you needed to have works as well as the basis of your salvation, or at least as a contributory factor, if not as the main factor. That is a soul-destroying doctrine, that we have to add anything to Christ or that we have to add anything to faith. The Word of God is very emphatic that the whole of a sinner's salvation is in Christ, and that the whole salvation and the whole Christ is received by faith. We don't have to bring anything of our own to make us acceptable to God. All we need is to have Christ.

197

The apostle James, on the other hand, is writing against those who we would call antinomians—those who were saying that, as long as you have faith in Christ, it doesn't matter how you live, it doesn't matter what works you bring forth in your life. That is also a soul-destroying doctrine—the idea that, as long as you have what you choose to call faith in Christ, you can live as you like. The fact of the matter is that sinners are justified by faith alone, by faith in Jesus Christ, but the faith by which they are alone justified, as is often said, is never alone. When we have that faith which alone justifies the sinner, that faith will be accompanied by works that are in keeping with the revealed will of God.

So there is no contradiction between Paul and James. They are both writing by inspiration of the same Holy Spirit of God. And whether our tendency is toward legalism or toward antinomianism, we need the full teaching of the Bible to put us right and to make us understand the truth that faith secures the salvation of the sinner without any contribution from any works of ours. But the faith which secures the justification of the sinner will always be accompanied by works that are the product of the Holy Spirit, just as the faith is the product of the Holy Spirit.

1. In looking at these words today, I would like to begin, as enabled, by noticing that it is a good thing to believe the truth concerning God. 'Thou believest that there is one God; thou doest well.'

2. But then secondly we have to recognise that there is a belief in the truth concerning God which can be had by the person who is still in a state of sin. 'The devils also believe, and tremble.'

3. The third thing that we would like to notice is that the person is vain and that faith is dead where faith is not fruitful in works. 'Thou believest that there is one God; thou doest well: the devils also believe, and tremble. But wilt thou know, O vain man, that faith without works is dead?'

1. It is good to believe the truth concerning God

Believing that there is one God is more than just believing that a God exists. It is more than just believing that there is a Supreme Being. It is more than just believing that there is a God, whatever description one might give to him, whatever characteristics one might apply to him. When the Bible speaks about believing that there is one God, or that God is one, it is bringing together everything that it has taught concerning the nature and character of God. When it speaks about God, it is not speaking about whatever people may choose to call God. It is speaking about God as he has revealed himself, as he has revealed himself in his works, as he has revealed himself in his Word, as he has revealed himself supremely in his Son, the Lord Jesus Christ. It is believing that all that is said concerning God in his Word is true.

He is the creator of all things. He created all things by the word of his power in the space of six days, and all very good. He maintains all things in his providence. He is causing all things to be accomplished according to his purpose. He is also the God with whom we have to do: our maker, our sustainer and our judge. He is the God who has given the law which is to govern our lives, the God against whom we have sinned, the God by whose justice we are condemned. He is the God who has chosen to redeem a people from this fallen race. He has provided a Redeemer in the person of Jesus Christ. The God that is spoken of here is not any kind of God that people may choose to fashion, but he is the God and Father of our Lord Jesus Christ.

It is a good thing to believe that God is, to have that conviction in our own minds and souls that what is written about God in the pages of the Bible is true, that this is the God who rules over all and this is the God with whom we have to do. If you remember the story of 'Rabbi' Duncan, he had gone through an agnostic and perhaps atheistic period in his early days. But when he was convinced that God is, he danced with joy on the Brig o' Dee near Aberdeen. And yet, he says that was just an intellectual enlightenment. But there was such satisfaction with coming intellectually to the enlightenment that

God is. We will never come to a personal relationship with God, a personal dependence upon God, if we don't come to an intellectual acceptance of the truth that God is. It is a very precious thing to be freed from doubts about the existence of the God of the Bible. These doubts assail people, and they assail some people more than others. They may assail those of a philosophical bent of mind more than they do others, although that is not always the case. But to be able to come to a steady conviction that the God and Father of our Lord Jesus Christ exists is a very real benefit. It is good. Thou doest well.

Some people see an element of sarcasm in what James is saying because he goes on to say that you are just like the devils—they believe that God is. But we can take the words just as they are written—it *is* good. It is right to believe that God is. We should be thankful today if we have even that real conviction concerning the existence of the God of the Bible and that we really believe that this is the God before whom we are soon to appear and render our account.

2. The unconverted may have a belief in the truth concerning God

Now we have to notice that there are those who have this conviction, who believe this truth concerning God, and yet they are in a state of sin. They are not converted. 'Thou believest that there is one God; thou doest well: the devils also believe, and tremble.'

There is not a devil in hell that does not believe every word that is in the Bible, as a matter of intellectual assent. That is true of the devil himself as well as of all the demons. The devil came to tempt Adam and Eve in the garden of Eden. He came to raise questions in their minds about the truth concerning God. The sad thing is that he knew that he was telling lies himself. He knew the truth concerning God. He knew that, when God said something, God meant it and God would do it. That is why he is called a liar from the beginning. It was not that he was ignorant—he was deceitful. There is no one better acquainted with the truth concerning God, intellectually, than the devil is. The eighteenth century American theologian Jonathan Edwards said concerning Satan that he was educated in the best divinity seminary in the universe, in heaven itself. The devil knows the truth about God, and the devil knew the truth about God when he was trying to deceive Eve and Adam into believing a lie concerning God. *All* the demons believe the truth concerning God. Some of the most straightforward statements concerning the divinity of Christ are found coming from the mouths of demons in the New Testament. 'I know thee who thou art, the Holy One of God' (Mark 1:24). 'Thou art the Son of God' (Mark 3:11). 'Thou art Christ' (Luke 4:41). They *believe*. They know what is true concerning God, intellectually.

What is more, what they believe has an effect upon them. They tremble! You can see that in the Gospels too. 'Art thou come hither to torment us before the time?' (Matthew 8:29). 'Art thou come to destroy us?' (Mark 1:24). The devil knows that the truth concerning God is fatal to himself. He knows that he will be destroyed because of his sin, and yet he keeps on sinning. He knew when he attacked our first parents that he was heaping up a burden of wrath for himself. He knew when he attacked Christ that he couldn't succeed in turning him away from the cross. So although the devils believe, although the devils tremble, it doesn't change their nature. It doesn't make them holy. It doesn't make them sue for mercy. It doesn't change them at all. They are still just as determined to go on in the ways of sin.

The devil is a great mystery, when you think of him. He knows the truth concerning God. He knows his own destiny as a fallen angel. He knows that every sin he commits is adding to the weight of his guilt and his condemnation, and yet he is so set upon the ways of sin that he will persist in these ways, whatever the consequences may be.

That just shows that there is a belief in the truth, an intellectual acceptance of the truth, whether willingly or unwillingly, which leaves a person basically unaffected, basically unchanged. A person may have more knowledge than many professional theologians, and be more assured of the truth of these things than many professional theologians today are, and yet they may go on in unbelief and go on in sin, intellectually saying one thing, but practically saying another.

This is being mentioned by James so as to impress upon his readers the fact that we need something more than just that good intellectual acquaintance with the truth. We can have that acquaintance and we can have that measure of acceptance, and yet that will not break the power of sin. That will not break the love of sin in our hearts. The most wicked person might have strong convictions regarding the truth of what is written in the Bible. Whether it makes that person tremble or not is something else. But there is a warning there that we can go on in sin and we can go to a lost eternity over the strongest convictions of the truth and over the most awful shudderings on account of the truth. We need more than to be intellectually enlightened in the truth. We need more than to be shaken to the core of our being by the truth. The devils also believe and tremble.

That is a thought for us today. Probably we all believe that the Bible is the Word of God and that what it says about God is true. What it says about any subject it deals with is true. Perhaps there are times when some of these truths have made us tremble. Maybe you can remember trembling under the Word of God and wondering, 'What is going to become of me if these things are true, as I believe they are?' What is going to become of me? And yet you go on in unbelief and impenitence and disobedience to the truth.

3. Faith without works is dead

The third thing—the main thing perhaps—is that the person whose faith is nothing more than the faith that even demons have, is a vain, empty person, and that person's faith is dead. 'Wilt thou know, O vain man, that faith without works is dead?' If faith is unproductive in the life, then that faith is dead, and the person who has that faith is vain, empty, and has got no spiritual substance or reality at all.

The Bible lays great stress upon faith. 'What must I do to be saved? Believe on the Lord Jesus Christ, and thou shalt be saved'

(Acts 16:30-31). We are justified by faith. The faith that saves—the faith that justifies—is faith in Jesus Christ. The virtue is not in faith itself, but in the object of faith. That is a matter of great importance, to remember that the virtue is in the object, and not in the faith itself. Faith may be strong, or faith may be weak, but as long as faith is the reception of Jesus Christ and resting upon him, that faith saves because the salvation is in Jesus Christ. He is made unto us by God wisdom and righteousness and sanctification and redemption (1 Corinthians 1:30). The faith that saves is faith that receives Christ. It receives the truth concerning God, as that is revealed in his Word, and it receives Christ, who is revealed in that truth as the only Redeemer of God's elect.

This is the great difference between a merely intellectual assent to the truth, however sincere that assent may be, and saving faith, which actually entrusts oneself to the Saviour who is set forth in the truth. It is a receiving and resting upon Christ alone for salvation. It is taking to ourselves what is offered to us in the gospel of Jesus Christ. There is this personal appropriating of Christ, this personal reliance on Christ for salvation. That is what makes all the difference between the faith that is alive and the faith that is dead. It is a good thing to assent to the truth intellectually, but we need to receive that truth into our hearts, into our minds. It has to influence our will, it has to influence our conscience. The Saviour whom it sets before us has to be welcomed—received by the soul so that the soul comes to depend on Christ alone for salvation, to abandon all other grounds of confidence and to put confidence only in the Lord Jesus Christ.

That is the faith that James is speaking about. In fact, he says in verse 14, 'What doth it profit, my brethren, though a man say he hath faith, and have not works? can faith save him?' What he is saying is, 'Can that kind of faith save him?' It is saving faith he is talking about, and he is emphasising that saving faith will be accompanied by, and it will be fruitful in, good works. Faith without works is dead, it doesn't really exist at all. James is not bringing faith and works together, as if they were sharing the work of salvation between them, but he is talking about a faith which is productive of works. Faith in Jesus

Christ alone saves the soul, and that faith is always productive of works, of *good* works.

Paul was saying the same thing when he was emphasising so strongly in the Epistle to the Ephesians the place of grace and the place of faith in the salvation of God's people. 'By grace are ye saved through faith; and that not of yourselves: it is the gift of God: not of works, lest any man should boast. For we are his workmanship, created in Christ Jesus unto good works, which God hath before ordained that we should walk in them.' (Ephesians 2:8-10). You see, that is the order. I know I am speaking about things that are very basic, and things that we all know, but they are things which we all need to take to heart. We are saved by grace through faith, not of works. But we are his workmanship, created in Christ Jesus unto good works. That is the order. It is not works that we bring to God, even *along* with faith, but works that are consequent upon God bringing us to himself through Jesus Christ by faith.

James is just taking up that same truth and emphasising what, as he was inspired by the Holy Spirit, he felt needed to be emphasised to the people with whom he was dealing. That is, while you cannot bring any works to Christ or to God as a basis of salvation, if you come to Christ, if you come to God through Christ by faith, the faith you have was given to you by the Spirit of the living God. The same Holy Spirit who creates faith in the souls of sinners creates along with it what the Shorter Catechism calls 'full purpose of, and endeavour after, new obedience.' It produces in the soul a concern to live in a way that is in keeping with the revealed will of God. You find that, for example, when Paul was writing to the Thessalonians, what he saw as a sign of the reality of their conversion to Christ was the fact that their faith was working. 'Your work of faith and labour of love' (1 Thessalonians 1:3). That is what showed that their faith was real. It was productive in their lives.

One needn't wonder at that, when you think of the fact that God the Father's purpose in providing salvation for sinners was that they might be holy. The apostle Paul, writing to the Ephesians, again brings that out, that this was the purpose for which God chose to save sinners, 'according as he hath chosen us in him before the foundation of the world, that we should be holy and without blame before him in love' (Ephesians 1:4). God the Father wanted to create a holy people, a people devoted to him, a people whose lives would be conformed to his revealed will.

That is the purpose that the Lord Jesus Christ had in coming into this world and rendering obedience in the place of his people and suffering for them. His purpose was to secure a holy people—not just to save them from the *guilt* of sin, but to save them from the *power* of sin. That is what happens when sinners are brought to Christ, when they exercise faith in Christ. They are not just looking for deliverance from the guilt of sin. They are not just looking for deliverance from the consequences of sin. They are looking for deliverance from sin itself, from its power, from its pollution and from its presence. Jesus Christ died in order that sinners would be brought to God, in order that sinners would be sanctified and devoted to God.

That is also the purpose of God the Holy Spirit when he comes to work in the souls of human beings. He comes to renew them. The Spirit of the Lord is given in the washing of regeneration and renewing of the Holy Ghost (Titus 3:5), so that people would be transformed, so that they would be enabled to present themselves as a living sacrifice to God, so that they would prove the good and acceptable will of the Lord in their own experience (Romans 12:2).

So we see that the work of the Father and the Son and the Holy Ghost is aimed at producing a people who devote themselves to works of godliness and holiness, who love the Lord their God with all their heart and soul and mind and strength, and who love their neighbours as themselves—whose love is not unproductive love, but love that finds practical expression in works of devotion to God and benefit to their fellow men. This is the emphasis that James is making here when he says that faith without works is dead. If faith was alive, it would be manifesting itself in works conformed to the will of God.

Now James is not saying these things just to put people down, but he is saying these things in order to summon them—to summon us—to the better way, to the exercise of a faith which is productive. 'Wilt thou know, O vain man, that faith without works is dead?' If you think you've got faith and it is not producing fruit in your life, you are really a vain person, an empty person, and your faith is dead. But he says, 'I am bringing this to your attention. Will you not know? Will you not face up to this truth? Will you not accept it and seek a remedy for the situation?' There is an appeal in these words. That's what is true concerning all the warnings of Scripture, even when they are put in a negative form: they are there in order to bring truth to bear upon the reader.

For example, we were considering on Sabbath morning recently how the Lord draws people to himself with the cords of a man, with the bands of love (Hosea 11:4). There is so much about the Bible and so much about God's dealings with sinners that is a drawing of them. Sometimes it is a gentle drawing, a wooing of them, a winning of them. How thankful we should be for those aspects of the Scriptures, of the gospel—that the Lord is attracting people to himself and to the right way. But sometimes the Lord has to use other methods to bring about these purposes of love. In Hosea he uses the illustration of the animal being drawn along and being encouraged by the yoke taken off it and food given to it and so on. But there are times when a goad, a prod, has to be used in order to get the beast to move. It is like that with us. There is so much that is encouraging us, so much that is drawing us, so much that is wooing us to Christ, and to the life of faith and godliness. But sometimes we need a prod, we need a goad, we need a sharp experience to make us face up to the dangers we are in, to make us face up to the reality. That is what James is giving to us here. Wilt thou know, O vain man? Will you not face up to the fact that your faith is dead? It is not real at all if it is not productive. Will you not seek to have that faith which *is* productive of good works, the faith of God's elect, the faith that is the gift of God, the faith which we are urged and exhorted to exercise?

Although it is put in a negative form, James's question here is an appeal. If you will not listen to the truth coming from one direction, will you not listen to the truth coming from the other direction? If you won't be drawn to faith in Jesus Christ, will you not be driven? Will you not face up to the serious situation of being without a fruitful faith?

That is really the question that is facing us today. Do we have the faith that produces works, the faith that gives us a longing and endeavour after holiness, the faith that makes us want to be conformed to the will of the Lord, to do his will in our lives? Will we not see the danger of having a faith which is intellectually satisfying but spiritually and morally unproductive? That is what was the case with many of James' readers, and it can be the case with us. We can settle down, satisfied that we believe everything that is written in the Bible from beginning to end, we believe the truth concerning Jesus Christ, we would defend it against those that attack it. But the question is, do we really believe it ourselves in such a way that we trust in the Saviour who is set before us in it? We adhere to the doctrines of the Bible. They are often described as Calvinistic, and there is something extremely intellectually satisfying about the Calvinistic understanding of the doctrines of truth, and people with an intellect of that kind can find satisfaction in these logical doctrines. We have to ask ourselves, while everything we believe is true, is our belief itself a true, soul-transforming, soul-saving faith in Jesus Christ? Do we have a faith that will survive the challenges of life and death and judgment and eternity? I think it was Lachlan Mackenzie of Lochcarron who said that the streets of hell would be paved with heads that were full of the knowledge of the truth. We have to beware of that. It is a good thing to know the truth, it is a good thing to be intellectually satisfied with the truth. But if the truth is to save us, if the truth is to make us free, then we have to receive it by faith, we have to receive Christ by faith, and by a faith that is proved to be alive by the influence that it has on our lives.

So the big question is really the old question, 'Dost thou believe on the Son of God?'

May the Lord bless his Word.

O Lord, we thank thee that we have been brought up and that we live in the light of the truth of thy Word. We pray, O Lord, that we might absorb that truth and that it might be believed by us, not only intellectually but also in a way that causes us to receive Christ, to embrace Christ, and to rest upon him alone for salvation, and in a way that transforms our lives. We pray, O Lord, that thou wilt sanctify us through thy truth: thy Word is the truth. We pray that we will give heed to the counsels and the warnings of thy Word, and that we will not rest without a personal acquaintance with Jesus Christ, the eternal Son of God. We pray that thou wilt part us with thy blessing, and be with us throughout thy day, and come out with us in the evening, if that is thy will. Take away our many sins. For Jesus' sake. Amen.

Concluding psalm—Psalm 119:33-37

14

How long halt ye between two opinions?

1 KINGS 18:21

And Elijah came unto all the people, and said, How long halt ye between two opinions? if the Lord be God, follow him: but if Baal, then follow him. And the people answered him not a word.

LORD'S DAY EVENING, 14TH AUGUST 2011

As you know, the Israelite kingdom was divided after the death of Solomon. The section that departed was known as Israel, and it had a succession of wicked monarchs. The worst of them all to date had been Ahab's father, Omri. But Ahab went even further than Omri. Ahab led the people further into the worship of Baal. There were many Baals—'baal' was just the word 'master' or 'lord'. Every place had its own lord. (You see the plural of the word there, baalim.) At this time, Baal had great influence in Israel through the marriage of Ahab to Jezebel, the daughter of the king of Tyre—it was the same Baal that was worshipped in Tyre that was worshipped in Israel. The worship of Baal was countenanced in the royal court, a place of worship was set up in Samaria. And the forces of the crown were used to persecute the prophets and preachers of the Lord. There is no doubt that those who feared the Lord in Israel were greatly intimidated, and were conducting their worship of the Lord to a large extent in secret, because even Elijah didn't seem to be aware that there were seven thousand who had not bowed the knee to Baal.

By the time of this incident, the nation had suffered for three and a half years with drought and famine, brought upon them by the prophet of God. And although Baal was the god of nature, the god of the fertility of the soil, he was not able to reverse what God had done. You would think that three and a half years later the people would come to their senses and realise that they were under the judgment of God, that the false gods they were worshipping were not gods at all. But instead of acknowledging their sin, they only tried to find ways around their trouble. You see that with Ahab. Instead of acknowledging his sin and seeking God's mercy, he is sending people all over the country, looking for water to keep the beasts from dying.

Modern man is not so modern after all, because we are seeing the same thing this last week [in the London riots, 6th to 9th August 2011] and in the last years, in our own nation. There is a failure to grapple with the fundamental problem of society, which is human sin, and a looking for solutions which, however varied they are, do not take account of God. Human nature is the same, whether it is thousands of years before Christ, or whether it is today. The carnal mind is enmity against God, and the last thing sinners will do is acknowledge God in repentance and in faith.

But now the time has come—God's time has come—to face the people with the challenge, with the choice. 'How long halt ye between two opinions? If the Lord is God, follow him, but if Baal is God, follow him.' The prophet is not suggesting that it is a matter of choosing what pleases you. He is not suggesting that they are just as entitled to choose the one thing as the other. He is pressing the claims of God and calling upon them to face up to the stupidity as well as the wickedness of worshipping a god who cannot hear and who cannot speak and who cannot do anything.

As enabled, I would like to say a little about three things.

1. The condition of the people—they were halting between two opinions

2. The demand of the prophet, which he made in the name of the Lord—a demand coming from heaven through the prophet

3. The response of the people: 'not a word.'

210

1. The condition of the people

There were two opinions among them: two philosophies, two religions, two ways of thinking, two ways of living. There were many of the people who were halting between these opinions. They were limping along, not knowing what side to come down on. On the one hand, is the Lord God? Or on the other hand, is Baal God? The Lord, as I tried to mention already today, is a term that includes everything that has been revealed about God in his Word. It is not just this concept of there being a God who is supreme, but the God who is supreme is the God of Abraham and Isaac and Jacob, the God of Moses, the God of David. He is the God and Father of our Lord Jesus Christ, the God who sent redemption to his folk, the God who is in covenant with his people. He is the Lord, and the question they have to face is, are they recognising him as their God? Do they acknowledge, do they worship, the one living and true God? That is the one theology, the one religion, the one opinion.

On the other hand, there is Baal. Baal is a conception of the human mind. 'All the gods are idols dumb, / which blinded nations fear' (Psalm 96:5). If people will not worship the one living and true God, they have to replace him with something else in their lives. It may not be in that primitive way of making idols of stone and of wood—we read in the New Testament that covetousness is idolatry (Colossians 3:5). But we are looking for something to replace God—sometimes it is in philosophy, sometimes it is in theology, sometimes it is just in the practical life of the sinner. Looking for something—we need *something*. Man was made for God, and if man will not worship God, he will worship something else. There is no doubt about it. Some people are making a god of the very denial that there is a God. They cannot get away from God, and they spend their lifetime trying to demolish the idea of God. They are making an idol of their own atheism or their own agnosticism. They are making that determine the course of their life. If Baal is god, then follow him! You see, there was this opinion that these false projections from the human mind were God.

These are the two opinions that are set before the people here, two ways of thinking about God. Either the Lord is God, or something else is God. That is true of you and of me here tonight. If we are not worshipping the one living and true God, then there is something else that has taken his place in our lives.

Now they were halting between these two opinions. There were many people there who were quite decided in favour of Baal—for example, the prophets themselves, and the king, and no doubt many of the people—because the religion of Baal allowed people more or less to live as they liked. That is a great attraction to the sinner, to be left to live as he likes. The god that will allow that is going to be very popular.

So there were people who were decidedly for Baal, and there were others—and we have only information about one of them here, Elijah—who were decidedly for God. He had no doubt about who God is. He was quite open in affirming who God is. He was quite prepared to take all the consequences that followed on affirming that the Lord is God. So we mustn't think that *everyone* was undecided. There were some who were really decided on the side of Baal, and there was at least one who was really decided on the side of the Lord. There were others in Israel—I mentioned already, seven thousand of them—and their decisiveness on the side of the Lord couldn't have been so obvious as Elijah's was. But the mass of the people were halting between two opinions.

When we try to think of what sort of categories there would be within that mass of people, no doubt there were those who knew that the truth concerning the Lord was truth indeed. They knew that what they had been taught was the very truth of God, that there is one living and true God, and that he is the God of Israel. They had the books of Moses, and they had the revelation of God's will for them and for their lives, and yet their heart went after the world and the flesh and the devil. They couldn't give themselves altogether to a life of sin because they were held back by the conviction that the Word of God is true and that the Lord is God. But they would not give themselves to the Lord, and they could not give themselves just as entirely as they would like to the world either. They were halting between two opinions, trying to unite the worship of God with the service of Baal. We read elsewhere of the people who later gathered into Samaria, that they feared the Lord, and served their own gods (2 Kings 17:33). They had some sort of recognition of God, and yet the real service of their lives was given to things that were not God. So that was one type of person, we believe, that was halting between two opinions.

Then you get the other kind of person, and that person is going in the ways of sin and in the ways of Baal and the ways of the world, and would like to do so even more, but there is this nagging in the mind and in the conscience. Perhaps the Lord is God. Perhaps the Word of God is true. I think there must be many people who are brought up under the sound of the gospel, and that is the way it is with them. They would love to give themselves wholly to the ways of sin. That is the predominant concern, to throw off the shackles. But they have this fear: perhaps God does exist, perhaps the Word of God is true.

It is just a difference of emphasis. There is the one kind who is following the ways of the Word, but would like to follow the ways of the world. Then there is the other one who is following the ways of the world, but is afraid that there is something in the truth after all. These were the ones who were halting, and one might say that to some extent about the seven thousand. We cannot condemn them. Elijah was in a depressed condition when he said that he alone was left, so that we can't put too much stress on it, but we can say at least that there are times when the people of God are not sufficiently decisive in their attachment to him to be out and open, whatever the consequences, in their following of the Lord. They are halting. They want to walk in the ways of the Lord, but the fear of man brings a snare, and other things take possession and keep them from being as out and out as they would like to be for Christ and for the gospel.

Well, that is just a glance at the sort of situation that Elijah is addressing. It is a great multitude of people, and many of them are in this state of being pulled both ways. Some of them are being pulled more in one way than the other, but the result is that they are neither one thing nor the other. They are neither entirely for God nor entirely given over to the ways of the world. However, one thing we must say about a person like that is that there is no doubt that they are really on the side of the world and the flesh and the devil.

2. The demand of the prophet

Elijah makes a demand. He says, 'How long halt ye between two opinions? If the Lord be God, follow him, but if Baal, then follow him.' When Elijah says 'if,' he doesn't mean that there is any uncertainty in his mind as to the fact that the Lord is God. There is no question as to who God is, and he is not suggesting that people are free to make up their own minds in the matter. No one has the freedom, no one has the right, to reject the authority of God. Whatever liberty, whatever rights people have, they have no right to reject God. They have no right to choose the ways of sin. Elijah is not suggesting that for a moment. And he is not suggesting that the outcome depends on the majority vote, as if people can determine who shall be worshipped as God. That is the state we ourselves are getting into as a nation. Instead of firmly standing for the truth that the Lord is God, there is this tendency to pay attention to the voices of the people and to give equal status to false religions. There is nothing like that in what Elijah is saying.

Instead Elijah is calling on people to face the facts, to face up to the reality. If the Lord is God, then follow him. Think out the consequences, and think out the consequences of following Baal. Can you really follow Baal? If you follow Baal, there is nothing but confusion and destruction. Now he is calling upon the people to be decisive.

We strongly avoid the terminology of making decisions for Christ, because that terminology is associated to such an extent with Arminian evangelism and with the idea that people themselves have the power to turn to the Lord, as if you are at a polling station and you can make your choice. The Word of God makes it very clear that the sinner left to his own choice, left to his own will, will certainly not decide to follow the Lord.

But when there is a gracious, God-given faith in Jesus Christ, it leads to this decisiveness. It means that the person is not in a state of uncertainty any more as to these fundamental truths, but is decided in his opinion, decided in his view of God. That is what the prophet is calling for—people who are decided, people who are definite, people who are not vague in the views that they entertain concerning God and concerning the way of salvation, a people whose minds are made up and who are prepared to follow through the mind to which they have been brought by God in his grace. The prophet is calling for *decided* people of God, people of God who know what they believe, and people of God who will stand by what they believe, and people of God who will follow out what they believe in their lives.

'If the Lord be God, follow him.' If you really do believe that he is God, if you have that belief which involves you in trust and commitment to him, then follow him! Let your belief find expression in your life! Don't be halting between two opinions, but be determined in your following of the Lord and your following of his Word, your walking in the ways of holiness! The Bible calls us to such decisiveness. You remember way back in the time of Moses, after the incident with the golden calf. Moses said, 'Who is on the Lord's side? let him come unto me' (Exodus 32:26). Who is on the Lord's side? Let him come out into the open! Let him acknowledge that he is the Lord's! Let him stand up for the Lord!

You have something similar with Joshua, when Joshua was calling on the people. He said in Joshua chapter 24 (verses 14-15), 'Now therefore fear the Lord, and serve him in sincerity and in truth, and put away the gods which your fathers served on the other side of the flood, and in Egypt, and serve ye the Lord. And if it seem evil unto you to serve the Lord, choose you this day whom ye will serve, whether the gods which your fathers served that were on the other side of the flood, or the gods of the Amorites, in whose land ye dwell: but as for me and my house, we will serve the Lord.'

The Lord Jesus himself was teaching the same doctrines when he said, 'No man can serve two masters' (Matthew 6:24). No man can *serve* two masters. You cannot serve God and mammon. You have to be for one or the other. It is the same message. Paul, writing to the

215

Corinthians, said, 'You cannot be partakers of the Lord's table, and of the table of devils' (1 Corinthians 10:21). You can't be living for God and living for the world at the same time. This is what Elijah is pressing upon our attention, the necessity for being decisive in our following of the Lord. We need to have the right opinion, and we need to carry out that opinion into our lives.

And then he says, 'If Baal be God, follow him.' He is really calling on the people to face up to the situation. He is not saying to people, 'Just throw off all the restraints and live as you like if you are worshipping Baal.' It would be a great error to say to people, 'Either follow the Lord or give up any connection with his religion. Give yourself over to the world.' So many have done that. It is very sad to think of many people who had the privileges of the gospel, and today, as far as one can see, they are without any of the restraints that the gospel provides, and they are giving themselves over to sin. We mustn't think for a moment that there is any encouragement to that here. What he is doing is pointing out the tremendous distinction between following the Lord and following Baal, and the absolute necessity to follow the Lord, to follow him—not just to have the opinion that he is God, but to work that out in one's own life. The Word of God generally is summoning us to face up to these matters and summoning us to be decisive in our attitude to God and to his revelation.

3. The response of the people

The people answered him not a word. Not a word, not a sound came from all these people who were listening. And since they didn't say a word, it is very difficult to know what they were thinking. However, we can conjecture, when we transfer this to modern times and to any congregation confronted with the Word of God.

There is a silence. There is no response to be seen or heard. But we assume that there may be some—we hope there are may be some among them—and they are silent because they have been convicted in their conscience and they have been filled with shame and they don't think there is anything that they can say. They are rather like Job when he said, 'Behold, I am vile; what shall I answer thee? I will lay my hand upon my mouth' (Job 40:4). They are brought in guilty before God and not able to say anything. As someone has said, 'They could not defend themselves, and they would not condemn themselves, and therefore they kept silence.'

That applies even more to another class of people among them—those who kept silent because they were stubbornly rebellious against the Lord. If those who were filled with shame were silent because they could not defend themselves and would not acknowledge their sin, so also were those who resented what they heard and were stubbornly insistent on going on in their own way. They couldn't defend themselves, and they wouldn't condemn themselves. They just determined in their own minds, 'Whatever this prophet is saying, we are going to go on in the same way. We are going to go on in the ways which we have been following for years.' There are people who respond like that to the Word of God, to the calls and commands of that Word. There is a sort of stubborn silence. They are not prepared to contradict, but neither are they prepared to acquiesce in what is being said.

So there is the silence of those who are ashamed, and the silence of those who are resentful and who are determined to continue in their own ways whatever the prophet says. There is also a silence that indicates a lack of sensitivity to the word that is being spoken: neither ashamed nor resentful, but just indifferent. I think all of these responses to the Word of God are found where the gospel is preached. There are those who, especially at times when they hear the gospel, feel they cannot say anything to defend themselves against its accusations. They cannot say anything to deny what it has to say about our need of it and the provision that is there for sinners in it, but they just remain in silence. There are others who resent the Word, who rebel against it. They might feel the pricks of it at the time, but they are determined to go on in the ways of sin. There are others, and they might not have heard a word at all for all the effect that it has upon them. They have nothing to say because they are not really concerned about the matter.

Well, we are many centuries—millennia—after Elijah's day. But has anything really changed when it comes to human nature, and when it comes to sinners and their attitude to the Word of God and to God himself? We have the same situation today. The Word of God is calling on sinners to believe the truth concerning God and to believe it in such a way that it influences the whole of life. There are some who, by God's grace, receive that admonition. There are others who do not.

But we mustn't think that the Bible presents these things to us in an indifferent manner, as if it doesn't matter really to us whether people respond believingly, obediently, or not. No, God is commanding sinners to repent. His messengers are beseeching sinners to repent. There is an urgency in the matter, and you can sense that urgency in Elijah's voice. How long halt ye between two opinions? How long are you going to go on in this unsatisfactory way? When will you come to your senses? When will you face up to the reality of your situation? When will you turn to the Lord in repentance? We have every encouragement in the Word of God to do so. God presents himself in the most attractive of lights to sinners. Yes, God presents himself as a consuming fire. He presents himself in the terrors of the law. He presents himself in all these awful threatenings as to what will come upon the ungodly, in order to persuade them to seek the Lord and to seek his mercy. But he also gives us such encouragements, revealing that he is a God of mercy, a God with whom there is forgiveness for sinners, a God who will receive those who turn to him—however long they have been halting between two opinions, however long they have been walking in the ways of the world. But the Lord is putting that before us with a sense of urgency. 'Seek ye the Lord while he may be found, call ye upon him while he is near: let the wicked forsake his way, and the unrighteous man his thoughts, and let him return unto the Lord, and he will have mercy upon him; and to our God, for he will abundantly pardon' (Isaiah 55:6-7). I just leave you with these words, 'How long halt ye between two opinions?'

May the Lord bless his Word. Let us pray.

O Lord, be merciful unto us. Make us thankful for all our gospel privileges. Make us thankful for all thy longsuffering and patience with us, and grant to us each the wisdom and the grace, the enabling to turn away from every false way and to put our confidence in thee. Grant us true repentance. Grant us true faith in Jesus Christ, the faith that leads the soul to follow him. Help us to follow thee fully, to follow thee all our days, so that we will be amongst those throughout eternity who will be following the Lamb as he leads them to fountains of living waters. Part us with thy blessing. Be with us in the week which has begun. Cleanse us from every sin. For Jesus' sake. Amen.

Concluding psalm—Psalm 86:8-11